africa pulse

STITCHING A WHIRLWIND

An anthology of southern African poems and translations

Translated by Nkosinathi Sithole, Biki Lepota, Tšepiso Samuel Mothibi, Stephen Masote, Koos Oosthuysen, Antjie Krog, Fred Khumalo, David wa Maahlamela, Gabeba Baderoon, Loyiso Mletshe, Zukile Jama, Johannes Lenake, Thokozile Mabeqa, Ncedile Saule, Rita Barnard

Co-ordinated by Antjie Krog
Edited by Megan Hall

OXFORD
UNIVERSITY PRESS
SOUTH AFRICA

OXFORD
UNIVERSITY PRESS

Oxford University Press is a department of the University of Oxford.
It furthers the University's objective of excellence in research, scholarship,
and education by publishing worldwide. Oxford is a registered trade mark of
Oxford University Press in the UK and in certain other countries.

Published in South Africa by
Oxford University Press Southern Africa (Pty) Limited

Vasco Boulevard, Goodwood, N1 City, P O Box 12119, Cape Town,
South Africa

Stitching a Whirlwind: An anthology of southern African poems and translations

ISBN 978 0 19 075420 4 (print)
ISBN 978 0 19 073748 1 (ebook)

First impression 2018

Typeset in Utopia Std 10pt on 15.5pt
Printed on 70gsm woodfree paper

Acknowledgements
Co-ordinator at the Centre for Multilingualism and Diversities Research, UWC: Antjie Krog
Publisher: Helga Schaberg
Project manager: Liz Sparg
Book and cover designer: Judith Cross
Typesetter: Aptara Inc.
Printed and bound by: Academic Press

We are grateful to the following for permission to reproduce photographs: Shutterstock/
GlebSStock/321802244 (cover); OUPSA/Admire Kanhenga (pp. 219; p. 220 Antjie Krog;
p. 223 JC Oosthuysen; p. 224); Zukile Jama (p. 220 Zukile Jama); CMDR (p. 220 Fred
Khumalo; p. 221 JM Lenake; p. 222 Thokozile Mabeqa; p. 223 Tšepiso Samuel Mothibi);
OUPSA/Helga Schaberg (p. 221 Biki Lepota); Rita Barnard (p. 222 David wa Maahlamela);
Stephen Masote (p. 222 Stephen Masote); Loyiso Mletshe (p. 223 Loyiso Mletshe).

The authors and publisher gratefully acknowledge permission to reproduce copyright
material in this book. Every effort has been made to trace copyright holders, but if any
copyright infringements have been made, the publisher would be grateful for information
that would enable any omissions or errors to be corrected in subsequent impressions.

THIS BOOK FORMS part of a series of eight texts and a larger translation endeavour undertaken by the Centre for Multilingualism and Diversities Research (CMDR) at the University of the Western Cape (UWC). The texts translated for this series have been identified time and again by scholars of literature in southern Africa as classics in their original languages. The translators were selected for their translation experience and knowledge of a particular indigenous language. Funding was provided by the National Institute for the Humanities and Social Sciences (NIHSS) as part of their Catalytic Research Programme. The project seeks to stimulate debate by inserting previously untranslated or neglected literary texts into contemporary public spheres, providing opportunities to refigure their significance, and prompting epistemic changes within multidisciplinary research. Every generation translates for itself. Within the broad scope of several translation theories, and the fact that one person translates differently from the next, it is hoped that these texts will generate further deliberations, translations and retranslations.

NATIONAL INSTITUTE
FOR THE HUMANITIES
AND SOCIAL SCIENCES

UNIVERSITY *of the*
WESTERN CAPE

Centre for Multilingualism
and Diversities Research

Contents

Foreword

You hold in your hands a South African collection of poetry in six African languages, both original and translations, that deliberates on the profundity of love, vividly evokes African landscapes, renders stringent judgements on apartheid and colonial cruelties, and carries a resonant philosophy of reciprocity. Its poems engage in an imaginative exchange *across* barriers of language, author and period, overcoming decades of riven conversations.

South Africans live in multilingual worlds, countering a limiting focus on English. Our region's languages reveal their mutual nearness through crossover words that act as connective tissue in our national culture (think of "boetie", "sisi" and "fundi"). Given this, translation should be our thirteenth language. Instead, our literary culture, publishing and education systems have not kept pace with this polyglot reality. Often as we advance in education, English catches us in a contradictory vice, offering much but demanding we abandon its fellow tongues.

Stitching a Whirlwind offers a return to linguistic neighbourliness and models a new relation between South Africa's languages. The collection necessarily decentres South African English, which lacks the wealth of sounds in Sepedi and Setswana, the incantatory lists and word-play of isiZulu and Sesotho, and the strong repetitions, gathering rhythms and wit of isiXhosa. These layered poetic meanings posed an intricate translational challenge and to do justice to them, the translators had to bend English toward its nearby tongues.

The translations reveal a tradition of virtuoso linguistic experimentation. For the authors included here, to write poetry is a grave and powerful responsibility. "It does not happen without happening", infers the visionary thinker SEK Mqhayi in "Sinking of the

Mendi", reflecting how even tragedy is part of the order of the world. In another poem of memory, LD Raditladi describes the undaunted South African soldiers reporting for duty in Europe during the Second World War as "Kgodumo-monsters of the thorn trees".

History threads through the poems, as in Nontsizi Mgqwetho's clear-sighted critique of colonial Christianity from an African Christian perspective in "The African waistcloth has fallen!" Similarly, Mqhayi's praise poem to King George VI of Britain is bracingly critical:

Here you come with a bottle and a Bible.

Here you come with a preacher arm-in-arm with a soldier...

Help us, O God, to which one should we yield?

– SEK Mqhayi, "Aa! Hail, Unsettling Country, you hero of Britain!"

Yet history is not always gratifying or redemptive. The shifting course of our complex past does not always align with contemporary views. The currents of history eddy, for instance, in "Chief Cecil Rhodes, the double-chinned one", a tribute by Neo H Kitchin. In this poem, Rhodes's expansionist vision grants British protection to some Africans, thus saving them from the incursions of the Boer Republics and the Germans.

Sometimes the poems mesmerizingly combine form and content, as though to try to alter history. In "The poems of Moshoeshoe and others: extracts" by DCT Bereng, a change of tense seeks to reverse the inevitable. Alternating lines in the present tense testify to the king's nobility, and endeavour to defer the inevitable ending to which the poem is building: "The sun snuffs its fierce power /... when we dig the grave of His Majesty", only shifting to the past tense in a much later line, "you have buried only the bones."

The relation to cattle offers an unparalleled source of poetic inspiration in the anthology. Allusions to curd, colostrum and whey convey a delectable intimacy. The speaker in OEHM Nxumalo's poem mourns "here they don't milk into their mouths – they pour from the bottle", suggesting the distance of modernity. In a fiery denunciation, Nontsizi Mgqwetho calls a new political party as lacking as "a cow with only droplets of milk, / that cannot even fill / the goatskin sack".

The fecundity of breasts suggests that the female body, both human and non-human, is not reduced to sexualised symbolism. Instead, as KE Ntsane's praise poem of the river "Mohokare" shows, breasts are symbols of strength, resoluteness and plenty: "Your mother is an Ndebele whose milk flows in easy abundance, / at her breast, many men have suckled". In fact, the power and abundance of breasts are not solely gendered as female. Compassionate men can be breastly, just as men can inhabit the subjectivity of a (female) cow. In "The shrinking and fencing in of the land", Yako writes about the impact of money in this way: "now we no longer lick each other like a cow licks her calf, / driven by love and inborn instinct. / Can one coin lick another caringly?" Expanding the range of portrayals of women, Princess Magogo's young lovers in "Hold me, hold me" and "Driving the days along" testify ecstatically about the men they adore, conveying a breathless female pleasure that is almost unknown in love poetry.

In the love poems, beauty takes innovative forms. For example, a woman is described both as "a magnificent hawk" and as a "calf-skinned daughter [who] shines gloriously" ("Beloved"). Cattle imagery helps to explain the varied allusions to skin colour across the anthology. Many poems refer as expected to the beauty of "your blackness, / which is like the beginning of night" ("Nomkhosi of my father"), yet skin ranges across a spectrum of colours in the poems.

While there are critical images of whites such as "Red-Scorpions" ("Modjadji") and "Those-with-Red-Beards" ("Black Wednesday"), positive references to a "lightness" of skin among black people occur in several poems. A close reading reveals not a desire for whiteness, but instead an aesthetic universe drawn from images of cattle, such as "the copper-skinned calf" ("Beloved"), to refer to the lustrous gleam of black skin. To describe someone through livestock metaphors also links that person to the ancestors. The exquisite young woman Pheladi is described as having a "golden complexion…suffused in milk, [who] absorbs the purest white from your mother's womb". But this theme holds another layer of meaning – of a sense of radiance within the body, as if glistening with electricity ("Moratuwa") from inside, suggesting the inner luminosity of a well-nourished and cared-for person. Thus, skin colour is described without defensiveness as "purest white", "lion-coloured", "tawny-skinned" and "sunburnt", a lexicon of beauty that was new to me, whose descriptions of skin were shaped by apartheid. Of course, apartheid did not leave this internal lexicon untouched. "An African" by AS Mopeli-Paulus shows what is at stake in views of blackness:

> my skin is the colour of my country –
> African child of the loamy black soil;
> For you also, the sun will rise
> – AS Mopeli-Paulus, "An African"

The anthology's translations were produced through a thoughtful and generative process. The roomful of translators who worked on the series did so mostly in solitude, but we also gathered in three workshops organised by Antjie Krog from 2016–2018. In these sessions, writers, translators and editors sat in companionable groups, often mulling collectively about words. This intensive and generous route has led to an anthology that begins to convey the wealth of the southern African poetic archive. Especially because archaic orthographies have long impeded access to the poems for modern readers, the excellent versions in *Stitching a Whirlwind* are an inestimable contribution to contemporary African literature.

I envisage a future in which this anthology is one among many, and crossings among South Africa's languages are ubiquitous, celebrated and widely read. There are hopeful signs. The student-organised InZync Poetry Project at Stellenbosch University has published a trilingual collection; and Rhodes University has a translation project on the work of five poets.

Poetry in translation can stem the leaching of our linguistic wealth into a narrow focus on English. If our childhood is filled with stories, poems and songs in a diversity of tongues, they remain ours in a profound way, and we can recover them even after an absence of speaking. *Poetry sings us*, and through poetry, we can embrace our heritage of many languages again.

Gabeba Baderoon
State College, Pennsylvania
June 2018

Introduction

This anthology gives readers a glimpse of the incredible depth and wealth of beauty, knowledge, flair and brilliance found in the literatures of indigenous languages in southern Africa. It is a selection of poems that the editor and translators hope will inspire a return to the many other texts not yet translated, to the original texts themselves, and a flurry of new and different translations.

The anthology forms part of a larger translation project, focusing on classical texts written in indigenous languages, which was carried out in the Centre for Multilingualism and Diversities Research at the University of the Western Cape, and kindly funded by the National Institute for the Humanities and Social Sciences.

Due to factors ranging from access to original texts and copyright, to funding and the availability and preferences of translators, this anthology cannot claim to be comprehensive or representative. Funding enabled the project to focus on poetry written in five languages: isiXhosa, isiZulu, Sesotho, Sepedi and Setswana. A few years ago, the senior staff of the Department of African Languages at the University of South Africa made a choice (for another translation project) of what they thought some of the best poems in their languages were. Among those who had suggestions in 2002 were Professors Bheki Ntuli, Ncedile Saule, Maje Serudu, Johannes Lenake, and Mr Mpho Mothoagae. Although only a fraction of those suggestions made it into the final translation stage, the bulk of the poems in this anthology come from that selection.

Over the years, the work of a few isiXhosa and isiZulu poets especially have been translated into English and Afrikaans; from these texts, more poems were selected and translated anew.

So the selection here does not pretend to be comprehensive or representative of the best poets, the best poems, the best translations or what is happening in all the South African languages. It is instead a handful of poems that we hope will inspire an honouring of the vast archive of literatures in African languages that have not yet been translated. From that revisiting, we hope, will come energetic projects of new and diverse translations, an expansive new readership, and vibrant discussion and engagement with our literary canon. But above all, we hope that the biographical detail, photographs, and the books themselves of the various authors and poets will be properly researched and gathered before some of them disappear for ever.

With translation, it is important to be aware of two established facts within the discipline of translation studies: first, two translators can translate the same poem at the same time and their versions would always differ, as the two versions published here of SEK Mqhayi's "The sinking of the Mendi" show. Second, to focus mainly on "equivalence" when translating poetry is to kill the poem's charisma, which is embedded in music and imagery. To be word-equivalent is to be untrue to the poem. In their best efforts, translators of poetry set themselves free to capture the beauty of the soul of the poem, rather than producing indisputable equivalents. This is why translators now often work in tandem: a mother-tongue speaker and a poet.

The original poems are published in this anthology with the English poems, not to suggest that the translation is equivalent, or should be equivalent to what is on the page next to it, but to enable speakers of the indigenous languages to experience an extra pleasure by reading the poem in the original. The orthography of African languages went through various manifestations during the past century. We have kept the orthography as it appeared in the version we were given, except in the case of isiXhosa, where the translators absolutely insisted on the most recent version – even for the poems of Mqhayi.

The poems were deliberately arranged in a way that moves them out of their language and cultural zones to enable them to properly speak to one another through English, and so cultivate new connections and enriched meanings. The style of each translator has, however, been kept.

This anthology is brought to you as a reader with all the goodwill, humbleness and longing of us as translators for indigenous poems to one day become an integral part of the South African poetry sound.

Antjie Krog
Coordinator of the translation project: Centre for Multilingualism and
    Diversities Research, University of the Western Cape, Cape Town
November 2017

Nomkhosi kababa

BW Vilakazi

Ngikuthandela ubumnyama bakho
Obunjengokuhlwa kobusuku,
Obukhanyis' amehlw' amakati:
Lawo mehlo ngawakho Nomkhosi.

Ngikuthanda ngesifuba sakho
Esiphakel' usapho lwakwethu
Ngobis' olumhlophe kuneliqhwa:
Iqhwa ngubuhle bakho Nomkhosi.

Ngokuthanda laph' usukhuluma
Sengath' ukhathele kawusathandi,
Namehlw' akh' enduluza phakathi
Emathunzini ezinkoph' ezinde.

Ngibon' ubuhle bezintokazi
ZakwaZul' ekade zakhohleka
Zafa; ngibubona bunyazima
Njengonyazi lusithwe zintaba.

Ukugqishazela kwakh' uhamba
Ukhathaz' insizw' iyokweshela,
Ikudlule qed' ikujeqeze
Ikubuk' ikhal' ezimaconsi.

Ngikuthandela unwel' ekhanda
Oluyimamb' emnyama yehlathi
Izibulunge ngemihluhluwe
Icwebezela njengamafutha.

Nomkhosi of my father

BW Vilakazi

I love you for your blackness,
which is like the beginning of night,
which lightens up cats' eyes:
those eyes are yours, Nomkhosi.

I love you for your chest,
which feeds my siblings,
the milk whiter than snow:
the snow is your beauty, Nomkhosi.

I love you when you speak
as if you are tired and don't want to,
your eyes moving inside you
in the shadows of long eyelashes.

I see the beauty of maidens
from Zululand who are long forgotten
and dead; I see it striking
like lightning hidden by the mountains.

Your firm steps as you walk
tire a young man courting.
He passes you and then takes a glance backwards,
watches you and tears flow.

I love you for the hair on your head,
a black mamba of the forest
with monkey-ropes coiled around its body.
It shines like fat.

Ngithand' amaziny' akh' anetsako
Ahlobis' umlomo njengentebe
Yeziziba zamanz' oThukela:
Sengathi kawudli nakudla.

Ngikuthanda nangezandla zakho
Engathi kaziliphath' igeja
Zigez' abantwana bakaNandi
Abaqhakaz' ubuhle njengawe.

Ngikuthanda ngakho konke kwakho
Name ngikukhonze kusengathi
Kawuzalwanga kulomhlabathi:
Wehla ngezilulu zamaZulu.

I love your teeth with their gap.
They adorn your mouth like an arum lily
of the pools of the waters of uThukela:
as if you don't eat at all.

I love you for your hands,
which look like they touch no hoe.
They bathe Nandi's children
who bloom with beauty like you.

Everyone loves you for all that is yours;
I worship you as though
you were not born on earth
but descended in heaven's basket.

Translated from isiZulu by Nkosinathi Sithole

Aferika

LD Raditladi

Lefatshe lena le lentle jang!
Le makhubu, ee, le dipala.
Le ditlharetlhare le majang;
Dikgama, dikgokong, diphala.
Phologolo tsotlhe tsa naga,
Kgatwane, kgwathe le dinoga,
Digagabi di ilang mariga,
Di aila fela mono Aferika.

Lefatshe le ke mosetsana,
Moratwa a thaka tse dikgolo,
Ntšwa fela a le mmala motšhwana,
Mmala o o bosulabogolo.
Selefera ke meno a gagwe;
Gouta ke marinini a gagwe;
Taemane dinala tsa gagwe;
Tsotlhe tse di mono Aferika.

Lefatshe leno la meriti;
La thunya di methalethale;
La dinoka di emang sesiti,
Di ikgarakgarang jaaka tlhale
Ke lefatshe la matlhomola,
Ruri fa go le letlhafula,
Fa dinku le podi di fula,
Diruiwa tsa mono Aferika.

Aferika, fatshe la letsatsi
Le phatsimang ngwaga fela otlhe;

Africa

LD Raditladi

This land, how beautiful it is!
It is with hills, oh yes, with plains,
with trees upon trees and grasses;
impala, wildebeest and springbok,
animals, animals of the wild,
lizard, leguaan and snakes,
reptiles that dislike winter,
they roam only here in Africa.

This land is an untouched girl,
loved by the great ones
because of her dark skin,
though to some the shade is a bad omen.
Silver are her teeth,
gold her glittering gums,
diamonds her nails;
all these are here in Africa.

This land of many shadows;
like a flower sprouting a kaleidoscope of colours;
place of meandering rivers,
weaving like a weaverbird.
This land is a tranquil land
truly, it never fails in summer
to allow sheep and goats to graze together,
the precious stock of Africa.

Africa, land of sun
radiating throughout the year;

Aferika lefatshe la metse
A masetlhana nokeng tsotlhe.
Lefatshe leno ke la temo,
Lefatshe leno ke la kgomo,
Lefatshe leno ke la khumo;
Tse di bonwa mono Aferika.

Lefatshe leno le lentle jang!
Le makhubu, ee, le dipala,
Le ditlaretlhare le majang;
Dikgama, dikgokong, diphala,
Phologolo tsotlhe tsa naga,
Kgatwane, kgwathe le dinoga,
Digagabi di ilang mariga,
Di aila fela mono Aferika.

Africa, land of water
drenching every river.
This land is of ploughing,
this land is of cattle,
this land is of wealth;
all of these are abundant in Africa.

This land, how beautiful it is!
It is with hills, oh yes, with plains,
with trees upon trees and grasses;
impala, wildebeest and springbok,
all animals of the wild,
lizard, leguaan and snakes,
reptiles that dislike winter,
they roam only here in Africa.

Translated from Setswana by Stephen Masote,
David wa Maahlamela and Tšepiso Samuel Mothibi

Pheladi

P Mamogobo

Ge ke be ke ralala le lefase ke butše mahlo ke tsomišiša ke tsoma mosadi yo nka tšhollelago maikutlo a ka a mpherehlago pelong, ke ile ka kganyoga Pheladi. Yena a ba thopa ya ka ka mmona ke hlologeletšwe lebaka le Pheladi e ka bago motho yo mogolo yo a ka amogelago tlhologelelo tša ka.

Pheladi yo mošwaana kunutu la pelo ya ka,
Pheladi ngwanana' Basotho phetathaga ya pelo.
Ke go bone kae ngwanana tšhikiriyamatswalo?
Ke gahlane nago kae wena tlhogohlamaikutlo?
O ntšeetše pelo o ntlholetše tshwenyego,
Bosamme kgaetšedi o ntlhadišitše
O nkgakišitše mme, Mologadi 'a Phogole.
Na o be o le kae ngwanana' bohlokwa?
O be o le kae tshehlana mantlhadišabagešo?

O nthopile pelo le maswafo
Botse bja gago bo nkubaretše
Bo ntšhetše ka fulalegolo fula la bothopša.
Mahlo a gago a bophaswana,
Ka mabala a swiswaletša bonaledi:
A phala bomphatlalatšane naledi mabonatšabošego.
Bošwaana bja gago bo medile
Bo tšwa teng bo boologa ka madi marwalabohlweka,
Bo phala bja ngwedi mahlapakamaru.
Ba go tšhetše ka bese la kgomobadimo,
Wa karabela o s'e mpeng bošweu bja tlepesela le setopo.
Ka hlaa le molokotsa a phala pitsi kobomabalabala,

Pheladi

P Mamogobo

*While travelling the length and breadth of the country, walking
with my eyes wide open in search of a woman onto whom I could
pour my feelings of love, I became pleased with Pheladi. She
captured me like a secret and I longed for the day when she would be
grown up enough to accept my desires.*

Pheladi, golden-skinned secret of my heart,
Pheladi, daughter of the Basotho, tiny royal bead of my heart.
Where have I seen you, beautiful arouser of my emotions?
Where have I met you, agitator of my emotions?
You have stolen my heart, I am left behind distracted,
you took me away from my siblings,
you have caused me to forsake my own mother, Mologadi 'a
    Phogole.
Where have you been all this time, precious girl?
Where have you been, tawny-coloured captivator?

You captured, you caught hold of my heart and lungs.
Your beauty has left me hypnotised.
It grazes, it wraps around me like a wave in captivity.
Your black and white eyes reflect the black and white of cattle loins,
they shine like stars:
they surpass the morning star, Lighter-of-the-Day.
Your golden complexion is deeply rooted,
coming from the inside, your beauty flows through your blood
    vessels,
it is purer than the moon washed by clouds.
You have been coated with the colostrum of ancestral cows.

Meetse letlapeng o nwa bjang nko e le lenono a' hlakane le
   mathaithai?
Molomo o nkurwana ke wa bagatša ba badimo,
Ka tsebe di magaketla o ageletša mehlamo ya badimo.

Pheladi, o nkutswitše pelo ka lerapo,
O otlologile sa ntshomolele ntshomathulathulwe,
O ganne mmelemosesane o kgethile mmelemabothabothe.
O betlilwe ke badimo mahlwa ba sa fele pelo:
Atla sa Raletatanana sa go tlamara matheka
Bana ba boa ka go swikaswikela manakaila:
Ka atlana tša masea ba otlolla mešifa,
Nala tša badulatagong tša ritela matheledi a tamangwana' kgoši.

O ntomeditše Pheladi morwedi wa badimo,
O nkgabeile o a nthemathemiša.
O ntlela bošego ke le boroko ditoro tša hlaba mokgoši wa gago,
Pelo e tutuetša riti sa gago go gopola šele go a pala.
Pheladi, ke wele pelo ke re: Pelo le maswafo o otlologile;
Ke kgotšwe sa mmaruri ke re: O mafahla mahlokasemenya,
O pelo maruthufaledi a tšatši la marega
O kgopololetago ngwedi tshehla' bošego.
Leleme o monate 'a koša' monyanya
Mantšu o nwega sa maswi a lebese.

Pheladi kunutu la pelo ya ka,
Tela kgapa sa pelo ya ka o ediga,
Tšhumella mahlahlo o tsošološe methopo pelong ya monna,
Rata o thibolle methopothopo ya nokana tša lerato,
Nka ke le ke adime pelo phegwana tša ramaebane
Ke phurume ke akelle bohlweka bja diba sa lerato,

Having been suffused in milk, your complexion absorbs the purest
   white from your mother's womb.
Your cheeks outstrip the zebra's softly dappled skin kaross,
with a nose so delicately pointed, how do you drink from the
   crevices of the rocks?
Your curved mouth is like that of ancestors' wives,
your elephant-sensitive ears enable you to receive all the messages
   from the ancestors.

Oh, Pheladi, you have stolen my heart like a dog steals a bone,
you are as tall as a sugar cane.
You rejected a slim body and chose a full one.
You have slowly and carefully been chiselled for me by the
   ancestors:
your beautiful hands sit comfortably on your waist
where children will keep arriving to stretch your sinews and joints:
with infant hands, they will stretch your muscles;
the shiny nails of the royal ones smooth your cheeks as smooth as
   those of the child of a king.

Dear Pheladi, you have greeted me, you, the daughter of the
   ancestors,
you have bewitched me; I swell like curd.
You keep on visiting me in my sleep where your calls pierce my
   dreams.
My shadow soul keeps following you as it is impossible to look
   away.
Oh, Pheladi, my heart falls down: your heart and lungs are open;
believing forever, I will keep saying: you are without sediment,
you are the heart that warms up a winter's day,
you are the bright moon that shines during the night.

Ke phephele ke pheme timo le kgadima di mello.
Pheladi yo mošwaana ngwanana yo botse le diatla
O lefa o sephiri khutamarama' pelo ya ka.

your tongue is as sweet as a wedding song.

Your words are as delectable as freshly milked milk.

Oh, Pheladi, secret of my heart,

you have kicked over the milk pot of my heart,

let the fountains rejuvenate a man's heart,

marry me and make the rivers of love flow freely.

Enable me to borrow your heart

so that I can fly over the fountains of love,

so that, splendid in myself, I escape great storms and thunders.

Oh, Pheladi, young one – even your hands are beautiful

you are my true inheritance, the secret treasure of my heart.

Translated from Sepedi by Biki Lepota

Lisholani?

Otty Nxumalo

Lisholani lelojuba,
Lisho lingabe lisanqamuka,
Lithi: "Amdokwe, amdokwe!"
Lisho sengathi liyangibona
Ukuthi sengilizwile ngililalele,
Lisho sengathi likhokha
Isibhongo sokuthi kade
Lalisho lingasangelameli, lisholani
Kabuhlungu, lingikhumbuza kude?

Lingikhumbuz' odadeweth' abalinde
Amabele kwelakwaMandlakazi, nabafowethu
Abacuph' izife emafusini.
Lisholani lingikhumbuz' oNgcazane –
Izinganekwane zogogo asebazithulela?
Lisholani lingikhumbuz' umcaba,
Izaqheqhe, nomlaza nesithubi?
Lisholani lingikhumbuz' amasi
Engangiwashiyelwa ngubaba uPhondolwendlovu?

Lapha kulindw' amakhekhe abhakiwe,
Kuxoxwa ngezithombe nebhola nomgqashiyo,
Abafana badlal' izimabuli namaphepha,
Bagemana ngemimese, ngenqindi nangezicathulo,
Lapha kudliwa amaswidi namabhloki eqhwa –
Lapha kudliwa ipapa nerayisi;
Lapha akuklezwa kuthululwa ibhodlela,

Why does it keep saying?

Otty Nxumalo

Why does that dove say,
keep saying without end,
"Amdokwe, amdokwe!"?
Saying it as though it sees
that I have heard it, that I am listening,
saying it as if it is taking
revenge because for so long
it sang without seeing me.
Why does it say it so painfully, reminding me, from far away?

It reminds me of my sisters,
waiting for the corn in the land of Mandlakazi,
and my brothers setting traps in the fields.
Why does it say so and remind me of Ngcazane,
the folktales of long-dead grandmothers?
Why does it say so and remind me of umcaba, sour milk,
the creamy umcaba, the whey and the colostrum?
Why does it say so and remind me of the umcaba
my father, Phondolwendlovu, used to leave for me?

But here we wait for biscuits that have been baked,
there's talk of film, football and umgqashiyo dancing,
boys play marbles and cards,
they hit each other with knives, fists, and shoes.
Here they eat sweets and ice blocks –
here they eat pap and rice;
here they don't milk into their mouths – they pour from the bottle.

Kungcono lithule lelojuba, ngoludala
Asisekuphinde sidle, sakubona sakubeletha!

Better that that dove keeps quiet!
We shall never again eat with the old spoon, woe unto us!

Translated from isiZulu by Nkosinathi Sithole

Ngibambeni, ngibambeni!

Princess Constance Magogo

Helele, helele! Awu, helele!
Helele, helele! Awu, helele!
Wamuhle lomfana, yeyeni!
Wamuhle lomfana, yeyeni!
Yeyeni, yeyeni! Yemama!

Ng'bambeni, ng'bambeni, bomama!
Seng' muka nomoya, yemama!
Seng' muka nomoya, yemama!
Yeyeni, yeyeni! Yemama!
Ng'bambeni, ng'bambeni, bomama!

Usebeyath' uyang'bheka ngamthanda!
Usebeyath' uyahleka ngamthanda!
Wayeyath' uyakhuluma ngamthanda!
Yeyeni, yeyeni! Yemama!

Wagibel' amahhash, amfanela!
Wagibel' elinsundu, lamfanela!
Wagibel' elibomvu, lamfanela!
Wagibel' elimhlophe, lamfanela!
Wagibel' iskemelo, samfanela!

Yeyeni, yeyeni! Awu, yemama!
Seng' muka nomoya, yemama!
Seng' muka nomoya, yemama!
Ng'bambeni, ng'bambeni, ng'bambeni!

Hold me, hold me!

Princess Constance Magogo

Helele, helele! Awu, helele!
Helele, helele! Awu, helele!
He's so handsome this boy, yeyeni!
He's so handsome this boy, yeyeni!
Yeyeni, yeyeni! Oh mother!

Hold me, hold me, mothers!
I'm being blown by the wind, mama!
I'm being blown by the wind, mama!
Yeyeni, yeyeni! Oh mama!
Hold me, hold me, mothers!

Whenever he looks at me, I love him!
Whenever he laughs, I love him!
Even when he speaks, I love him!
Yeyeni, yeyeni! Oh mama!

When he rides horses, they suit him!
He rides a brown horse, it suits him!
He rides a red horse, it suits him!
He rides a white horse, it suits him!
When he rides a horse speckled like corn beer sediment,
    it suits him!

Yeyeni, yeyeni! Awu, oh mama!
I'm blown by the wind, mama!
I'm blown by the wind, mama!
Hold me, hold me, hold me!

Translated from isiZulu by Nkosinathi Sithole

Uthando

CT Msimang

Uyimpicabadala weThabisile,
Uyinqabakayitshelwana weDuduzile;
Uyindida weBathandekile,
Uyinkinga weBazondekile;
Uyingwijikhwebu Bahlukanisile.

Ngikubonile ulumba inkomo edlelweni,
Yakhotha enye bathi ngeyikhothayo.
Ngisho nezinambuzane uzihungulile,
Izintothoviyane zaze zafa zibelethene;
Abantu bona bazethuke sebakhe emkhathini.

Nami wangithwebula ngandilileka,
Ngamfoma izithukuthuku kulel' ungqoqwane,
Ngakhangwa ukukhanya kumnyama khuhle,
Imamba nendlondlo zaphenduk' iziquzi,
Amagquma nezikhinsi kwaphenduk' amathafa.

Yebuya luthando unuka njengeqaqa,
Umuncu njengomhlonyane,
Ubaba kunesibhaha,
Uqanda kuneqhwa.

Love

CT Msimang

You are a riddle, Thabisile,
you are amazing, Duduzile,
you are confusing, Bathandekile,
you are a problem, Bazondekile,
you're a twist in the tail, Bahlukanisile.

I saw you enrapture a cow in the veld,
it licked another cow and then they nuzzled each other.
Even the insects you caught,
the locusts died one on the other's back;
and the people built castles in the sky.

You also hypnotised me till I was dazed,
I sweated while there was snow,
I saw the light when it was dark,
the mamba and horned adder turned into veld lizards,
hills and hollows turned into flatlands.

Oh love, you smell like a polecat,
you are as bitter as African wormwood,
even more bitter than a fever-tree,
you're colder than the snow.

Translated from isiZulu by Nkosinathi Sithole

Izibongo zikamaskandi

Bonginkosi Sikhakhane

Awu! Wazibamba uBonginkosi madoda!
Wazibamba umfo kaSikhakhane
Omnyama ngenkani.
Sazibamba isihosha sikaMazibani,
Sazibamba benyela abangizondayo,
Bahalalisa abangithandayo
Ngazibamba mina ngunguluzane
Okukade kwasa beyigunguluza
Abezibaya ngezibaya.
Wazibamba ugogo lo oyisimomoloti,
Ngingazange ngimbone ugogo oyisimomoloti
Ngazibamba mina bukhazikhazi,
Ubuhle bamabhodlela.
Ngazibamba mina siphuhlephuhle
Ophuhle phansi njengekhowe.

Bayangazi abaningi,
Umfula engiwuphuzayo
Ngiphuz' aMevane.
Khona kwesikaKhanyile isifunda.
Induna engiphethe nguMthethwa.
Khon' eThalaneni, KwaZulu eNkandla.
Usesho phezulu ezitezi umfo kaSigidla,
Unkomo zakhe zisesiswini
Ezabanye zisezibayeni.
Ubaba-ke ongizalayo lowo.
Ngizibambe naye umfo kaMzimela.
Khona phesheya kweNdikwe.
Khona KwaZulu eNkandla.

The praises of a maskandi singer
Bonginkosi Sikhakhane

Awu! Men! Bonginkosi plays them!
He plays the strings, this son of Sikhakhane
who is pitch-black.
He plays them, this hoarse-voiced son of Mazibani,
he plays them till my enemies feel ashamed,
and those who love me ululate.
I play them, I, Hard-Bitten-One
who has long been bitten
by those from many kraals.
He plays them, a chubby-cheeked old woman,
although I have never seen a chubby-cheeked old woman.
I play them, I, the sparkle,
the beauty of the bottles.
I play them, I, Sudden-Springer-Up
who sprang up like a mushroom.

Many know me,
I drink the river
called Mevane.
There in Khanyile's district
my induna is Mthethwa.
There at Thalaneni, at Nkandla in Zululand.
He plays in top-class buildings, this son of Sigidla,
he whose cattle are in his stomach
while others have theirs in the kraal.
That's my own father.
I am playing them with this son of Mzimela.
There across the Ndikwe.
There at Nkandla in Zululand.

Khuphuka Mnguni omuhle,
Ikhona lapho ingoma.
Hhawu! Yazibamba benyela ngempela
Ingunguluzane okukade beyigunguluza.

Come up, you beautiful Mnguni,
that's where the music is.
Hhawu! He plays them till they are humbled,
this hard-bitten one who has long been bitten.

Translated from isiZulu by Nkosinathi Sithole

Moratuwa

KE Ntsane

O teng mose wane sebakanyana,
Ke tswa mo tshwara ka ditsebe maobanyana.
Ka ema tseleng ka rakalla,
Ka rakalla sa nong le tshwere sebata,
Ka nna ka itula sefuba kgafetsa;
Pelong ka kokomoha ke se hlama borotho.

Thaba Qeme, kokobela
Ke bone kgunwana-kgubedu, ngwanabo Sesomo;
Kgaitsedi ya Jobo e dutse lebaleng,
E ntse e tidinya moropa e se lethuela;
Moropa ke wang lapeng la Tilane?
Moropa ke lerato fubeng sa thope.

Thope di tshohile tsa ka Leribe;
Thope tsa Leribe di tshositswe keng?
Tauhadi e teile mohala Bongalla,
E o otletse Matshekgeng habo Sepolo,
Ya re: "Ntebelle, ke a tla, Mokwena,
Bolella natshana di suthe tseleng,
Taba boholo di ngotswe tlapeng la Sekgowa."

Ha ke a ikgethela ke kgethetswe,
Ke kgethetswe kgubung, habo Thabang,
Ka kgethelwa ke kgosi di entse kgehlepe.
Kgehlepe ke yang, kgosana tsa Mokhachane?
Kgehlepe ke ya ngwana mokgubu wa 'Mmamokhachane.
Tilane o bebenyetsang ditedu lebitleng?
Tilane o tswetse tlakatshowana e se ho kgahleha!

Beloved

KE Ntsane

She sits over there some distance away,
I just held her tenderly by the ears to kiss a few days ago.
I stood there in the path stretching, twirling like a pumpkin plant,
I stood like a vulture, a predator on its prey,
and beat on my chest repeatedly;
in my heart I swelled though I am not bread dough.

Mount Qeme, subside!
So that I can see the copper-skinned calf, sister of Sesomo;
the sister of Job, she sits out in the open in the family courtyard,
she is beating a drum though she is not a diviner;
what is the drum doing in the family of Tilane?
The drum is love in the chest of a young woman.

Those young maidens of Leribe are scared;
those young maidens of Leribe, what scared them?
The great lion has sent a telegram to Bongalla,
he sent it to the land of the Matshekga, the home of Sepolo,
it said, "Expect me, I am coming, Mokwena,
tell those buffalo calves to get out of the way,
most of the news has been written on the slate of the whites."

I had no choice, she was chosen for me.
She was selected while still in the womb, at the home of Thabang,
she was chosen for me by the kings at a meeting.
What is the important news, princes of Mokgatjhane?
The big news is of the child of the navel of Mmamokgatjhane.
Tilane, why does your beard tremor from the grave?
Tilane, you have given birth to a magnificent hawk – your
     calf-skinned daughter shines gloriously.

Tsokotsane sa tsoha thotobolong,

Se fetela pelong ya ngwana a iketlile,

A hula korotjhe a loha kofia.

Tsokotsane sa pelo ya lerato sa lopalla,

Sa thulana le se ropohileng Botjhabela.

Basali ba beile matsoho diphatleng,

Ba ntse ba kgotsa bosawana kgafetsa.

Fubeng sa pati ke ngotse lengolo,

Tau e ngotse ngolo huku di pedi;

Pelo di pedi, rato le leng;

Ngwana ke koqohile pelo le matshwafo,

Ke ja jwang, ke a hlanya,

Ke hlantshwa ke rato la thope ditjhabeng.

Ha ke bue, ho bua sefuba;

Ha ke ithoke, ho ithoka lerato;

Nka ithoka jwang ke se kgeleke?

Tebong ba pelo ho dutse sekaqa,

Fubeng sa ka ho eme lefika,

Fika le ntse le qhibidiha se-ka-sereledi.

Leoto, nkuke o mpepe,

O ntshedise boPhuthiatsana madiboho;

Ka kwano ho Senqu ke kgahlilwe,

Ke kgahlilwe ke siba la mpjhe selailai,

Lailai se laimetse motwaitwai o dutse,

O dutse fateng sa moduwane o iketlile.

Ntho a nna nkuka ntsukutla,

Ntho a nna nkgothomeletsa pele.

A whirlwind rose from the ash heap,
it rushes to the heart of the girl who sits relaxed,
pulling the crochet hook, stitching a grass hat.
Stitching a whirlwind of love from the heart,
and merging with another one from the east.
Women shade their eyes looking into the distance,
they cry out in amazement.

On the chest of my girl, I have inscribed a letter,
the lion has written a letter with two cornerstones;
the hearts are two, the love is one;
little one, my heart and lungs are lifted up,
I eat grass, I am insane,
I am driven mad by the love of a young woman who stands out
    from among the nations.

I do not speak – it is the chest that speaks;
I do not praise – it is love that praises;
how can I praise when I am not a praise poet?
In the depths of my heart sits a lump,
in my chest stands a rock,
the rock is melting like butter.

Feet, lift me and carry me,
help me across the drift of the Phuthiatsana river.
On this side of the Senqu, I have been enchanted,
I have been enchanted by the lightning of a shining ostrich feather,
the shining one shines to the one who sits alone,
she sits relaxed by the willow tree.

Something takes me and jerks me,
something roughly pushes me forward.

Ngwana o tshwerwe ke kese diphakeng,
Methapo o fetohile kgole tsa lerato,
E fetohile masika a kese,
Masika a kese ke manqosa lerato.

Paki ha di yo, nnake kgaitsedi,
Paki ke pelo le matshwafo bobedi,
Ke tsona di letsang makotikoti sefubeng,
Makotikoti ke a ditshepe sefubeng.
Borokong tshepe di lla teuteu kgafetsa,
Teuteu ke ya lerato ngwaneng wa batho.

The girl is shocked by the electricity in my arms
the veins have become wires of love,
they have turned into sinews of electricity,
the sinews of electricity are the emissaries of love.

There are no witnesses, dear sister,
the witnesses are the heart and the lungs,
they are like tin-cans knocking together,
the tin-cans become bells in the chest,
even in sleep, the bells toll incessantly,
their toll is the toll of love for the child of gentle people.

Translated from Sesotho by Tšepiso Samuel Mothibi

Uze ungiphuzise amanzi

CT Msimang

Ngiyovuka kanye nekhwezi
Ngiphehle ubulawu obumhlophe,
Ngithake ngomthole novuma
'Ze ungithole ungivume.
Ngiyophuma nenhlamvu yelanga
Lapho ukusa kuqhakaze amazolo
Ngikubone uza, ukhashwa
Amakha amnandi kusasa;
Ngiyokulindela ngisemthonjeni,
Ngikulindele, ngikulindele.

Umoya wakho ngiwubone
Uphakama kunye nomlalamvubu
Kuphakame ithemba lami,
Lapho uthwele imbiza
Emnyama eyindilinga
Phezu kwekhanda eliyindilinga
Namehlo ayindilinga,
Nami ngawe ngiyadilingana;
Ngiyokunaka ngomnako wenyosi
Uze ungiphuzise amanzi.

Ngokhangela inxuluma lakwenu
Elitshalwe lamila entabeni;
Ngeke ngize ngimagange
Hleze ngibe ngisakhwele ngidilike,
Hleze ngiqanse imithambo,
Umqansa ungime esifubeni,
Ungikhendle ungigqib' ithemba,

Until you give me a drink of water

CT Msimang

I shall rise with the morning star
and stir up a white mixture of herbs,
I will mix in wild asparagus and palm fronds
until you find me worthy and accept me.
I will go out at sunrise
when the morning shines with the first dew.
I shall see you approach, escorted
by the fragrances of the morning;
I will wait for you at the spring,
I will wait, I will wait.

Your spirit I will see
rising with the thick morning mists.
My hope will rise likewise,
when you carry a clay pot
that is dark and oval-shaped
on your oval-shaped head
with its oval-shaped eyes.
I'm going round in circles about you;
I will distract you, like only a bee can,
until you give me a drink of water.

I will head to your extensive homestead
planted and grown on the mountain;
never will I come hastily
in case each time I climb I slip down,
in case my veins bulge,
the hill chokes my chest,
gets the better of me, buries my hope,

Nawe ungishingilele
Kumbe ungishalazele
Kumbe ungibhembesele.

Ngiyogcakela noNokubekezela
Nginqume negele noSineke;
Ngishaye ugubhu ngihaye
Ngivume inkondlo kaNomathemba
Ngigudle izintaba ngihaye,
Izintaba zingisondeze kuwe
Uyokuzwa inkondlo usexhibeni
Ingqongqoza esifubeni sakho
Ingqongqoze ingqongqoze
Uze ungivulele ngingene.

Wena ophezu kwezihlahla
Noma uphezulu kwelenyoni,
Inhliziyo iyonombela
Nomphefumulo ubambelele
Kuwo amagatsha emithi
Ngitibile ngizabalaze
Ngezikwepha zokunxanela,
Ngesibindi sokulangazelela,
Ngikunxuse ngikunxuse,
Uze ungiphuzise amanzi.

Wena ophansi ekjuleni
Ngiyojula ngithubeleze nami
Njengezimpande zomthombe
Njengomnyezane ngijule
Njengabavukuzi begolide
Njengabavukuzi bedayimane,

and you turn away from me
or shun me
or be cold towards me, unmoved.

No, patiently I will climb the hill,
meticulously I will cut the slope;
I will beat the drum and sing
reciting the poem of hope;
I will skirt the mountain and call out,
"Oh mountains, bring me near to you!"
You'll hear my poem in the hut
knocking on your chest:
it knocks and knocks
until you open and let me in.

You at the top of the trees
up there where the birds live,
my heart will climb,
my soul will cling
to the branches of the trees.
I will exert my strength and struggle
with the muscles of my burning desire,
with the valour of ardent longing,
I'll beg you, I'll beg you,
until you give me a drink of water.

You who are below all depths,
I will descend and burrow my path open
like the roots of the wild fig
like the roots of the willow, I will go down deep
like the gold miners
like the diamond miners,

Noma ngigqula phezu kwedwala
Noma izidladla ziqundeka
Ngikuqhwebe ngikuqhwebe,
Uze ungelulel' isandla.

Nakushisa, ngisho nakuqanda
Soze kungivimbele, phinde!
Isithwathwa esembeth' izintaba
Asinamandl' okukwemboza;
Naliqhwa nangqogwane,
Noma liza nesangquma
Noma liza nesiphepho
Siyongiphephetha singisondeze
Kuwe, ungibambe ngesandla
Unginike ukuphumula.

Wena ongaphesheya kwezilwandle,
Lapho umsinga udloba okwendlondlo
Namadlambi edlangile ngolaka,
Ngiyokweneka inhliziyo yami
Ibe isihlenga sokuwela,
Ngihlambe phezu kweJolidane
Ngiwele uLwandle oLubomvu;
Ezweni loju nobisi
Ngakhe khona nami
Ngibuse nami nawe.

Wena ongaphezu kwamafu,
Umphefumulo wami uyakuhluma
Umile izimpiko zokhozi
Ngimpampe phezu kwesibhakabhaka
Ngidabule amagagasi omoya;

even when I thrust against rock
even when the force of my muscles is blunted,
I will beckon you, I will beckon you,
until at last you stretch out your hand to me.

Whether it is red-hot or ice-cold,
Nothing will keep me away from you, nothing!
The frost covering the mountains
has no power to cover you;
even snow or ice,
even when the heavens rattle with hail,
even when the sky squalls down with stormy winds,
it will only blow me closer to you
so that you can grab my hand
and give me peace.

You who are across the oceans
where the whirlpool rages furiously like a horned adder,
where the waves lash with lashing fury,
I will spread my heart,
I will spread it to become a raft,
I will swim over the Jordan
and cross the Red Sea
to the land of honey and milk,
I will build my home
and live a bountiful life with you.

You who are above the clouds,
my soul will burst with blooms
and grow the wings of an eagle;
I'll wander across the universe
and slice through the waves of the wind;

Njengo-Elija wasendulo;
Ngigibele ingola yomlilo
Ngingqongqoze emasangweni ezulu,
Wena ongukuphila kwami
Ungivulele, ungivumele ngibuse.

and like Elijah of old,
I'll ride a chariot of fire;
I'll knock at the gates of heaven,
until you who are my life
open up and let me reign.

Translated from isiZulu by Nkosinathi Sithole

Umqhubansuku

Princess Constance Magogo

Maye, maye, babo!
Wo, yehheni!
Maye, maye, babo!
Wo, yehheni!
Muhl' uS'phikeleli!
Ngimthanda nje muhle, bo Zulu,
Ngimthanda nje muhle!

Mina loya munt' oza
Ngomzila wezinkomo nabantu!
Mina loya munt' ogijim'
Okhalweni ubong' layezela:
Umbomtshen' ubanin' nyakana
Mina sahlukana naye
Min' angiqond' ukuba
Ng' yaw' zenze njani –
Seng' yaw' z'shisela nendlu!

Ebuya, baba! Ebuya, baba!
Yebuya, baba! Yebuya, baba!
Ngimthanda nje muhle, bo Zulu,
Ngimthanda nje muhle!

Umntwana womuntu,
Mina nqiyamesaba
Umntwana womuntu:
Siphongo senyathi!
Umntwana womuntu:
Wumhluzi wempisi!

Driving the days along

Princess Constance Magogo

Dear me, dear me, father!
Wo, yehheni!
Dear me, dear me, father!
Wo, yehheni!
He's handsome, Sphikeleli!
I love him 'cause he's handsome, my people,
I love him 'cause he's handsome!

Here, to that man coming
along the path of cattle and people!
Here, to the person running
on the flatland – tell him this for me:
tell him
that if we ever break up
for my part, I don't quite know
what I'll do –
I'll burn myself in the house!

Ah, my father! Ah, my father!
Ah, my father! Ah, my father!
I love him for his handsomeness, my people!
I love him for his handsomeness!

A human child:
I am afraid to name him!
A human child:
the forehead of a buffalo!
A human child:
the gravy of a hyena!

Umntwana womuntu:
Wumsila wemamba!
Umntwana womuntu:
Wuphondo lwenkabi!
Umntwana womuntu:
Wumhluzi wengadula!

Umuhle yebuya nkaba,
Yakushon' esiswini!

A human child:
the tail of a mamba!
A human child:
an ox's horn!
A human child:
the gravy of a duiker.

You're so handsome with your navel
hidden deep within the flesh of your stomach!

Translated from isiZulu by Nkosinathi Sithole

Ingodusi

Gili kaNobantu

Phezu kweMfolozi,
Eduze neSikhwebeni;
Kwahlala ingodusi,
Yahlala njengenyosi,
Nsuku zonke ibubula:
"Way' eGoli, wayosebenza,"
Isho zigobhoza izinyembezi:
"Maye maye sowadliwa,
Kazi ngiyini emhlabeni,
Ngoba mtshingo ubethwa uba?"

Ekuphumeni kwelanga,
Iqalaze empumalanga;
Kumbe angayikhumbula,
Nangencwadi okaKhambule.
Ithumele umfana ingodusi,
Elayo alikho iposi:
"Way' eGoli wayosebenza,"
Isho zigobhoza izinyembezi:
"Akasabhali nencwadi encane,
Ngogana inyamazane na?"

Phezu kwetshe
Iphothula umcaba;
Phansi kweqanda lentshe,
"Mhlaba usicaba na?
Ungemdilingisi lapha na?
Angekhohlwe abuye na?
Way' eGoli wayosebenza,"

The promised girl

Gili kaNobantu

Above the Mfolozi river,
near Sikhwebeni,
sits a promised girl.
She moans like a lonesome bee,
everyday lamenting,
"He went to eGoli for work,"
as tears drop to the ground.
"Oh dear! Oh dear! He is taken,
what is to become of me?
must I be a reed pipe unplayed for ever?"

As the sun starts to rise
she turns to the east;
maybe he will remember her,
maybe the son of Khambule will write a letter.
The promised girl sends a boy to get the post –
no letter for her:
"He went to eGoli for work,"
she says, as tears drop to the ground.
"He doesn't write me even the smallest note,
will I have to marry a wild buck?"

On a grindstone
she grinds mealies for umcaba,
with a stone shaped like an ostrich egg.
"Earth, are you really flat?
Can't you bring him back to me?
Can't he forget and come back?
He went to eGoli for work,"

Isho zigobhoza izinyembezi:
"Makabuye noma angephuza,
Ngathela muva njengembumba."

Phakathi emasimini,
Kwenkulu imini.
Kukhala amakhaba;
Ifikelwe ukwesaba,
Sengathi wuye uyakhasa
Kwawommbila amakhasi.
"Way' eGoli wayosebenza,"
Isho zigobhoze izinyembezi,
"Akasangikhumbuli, cha!
Nokukhonza akasakhathali."

Ekuthambameni kwelanga,
Ekubuyeni kwezinkomo,
Lapho lavela khona ilanga,
Lapho zaphuma khona izinkomo,
Ziphinde zibuyele;
Yena akabuyi kuyona;
"Way' eGoli wayosebenza,"
Isho zigobhoze izinyembezi,
"Sowabhunguka, angeke abuya!
Sowabhunguka."

Phakathi elawini,
Ihlezi emunywini;
Izwa inja ikhonkotha,
Nomuntu enyonyoba;
"Akuyena othandwa yimi,
Kuphela umlamu wami:

she says, as tears drop to the ground.
"Even if I have to wait, let him return,
at least I will bloom even if belatedly."

Deep in the fields,
in the middle of the day,
tall plants start to rustle.
Suddenly, she is scared,
it could be him skulking
among the big-bladed mealie leaves.
"He went to eGoli for work,"
she says, as tears drop to the ground.
"He doesn't miss me any more!
He doesn't care to send greetings."

As the sun is fading,
as the cattle return to the kraal,
the sun returns to where it comes from,
the cattle return
to where they come from;
yet he doesn't return.
"He went to eGoli for work,"
she says, as tears drop to the ground.
"He has left me for ever, he will never return!
He has left me."

Inside her hut,
she sits in anguish;
hears a dog barking,
and somebody moving around.
"It is not my loved one,
it is someone who has come for my sister!

Way' eGoli wayosebenza."
Isho zigobhoze izinyembezi,
"Sowabhunguka, sowabhunguka!
Angeke esabuya!

Ebusuku kwamabili,
Phansi kwezingubo ezimbili.
lphuphe lifikile,
Yavuka lisukile,
Yabona ibiphupha.
Kakhulu yalingoza:
"Way' eGoli wayosebenza,"
Isho zigobhoze izinyembezi;
"Kungcono uhambe njalo,
Uzugugele eGoli!"

He went to eGoli for work,"
she says, as tears drop to the ground.
"He has left me for ever, he has left me for good!
He will never come back!"

At midnight,
covered with two blankets,
she sees him arriving.
She gets up – he is gone.
She realises it was a dream.
She sobs uncontrollably,
"He went to eGoli for work,"
she says, as tears drop to the ground.
"Better you never return,
till you're wasted in your eGoli."

Translated from isiZulu by Nkosinathi Sithole

Ukufinyezwa nokubiywa komhlaba

St John Page Yako

Batsho bon' abantwana begazi,
Noxa lon' ilizwe lingaselilo lethu.
Lo mhlab' uza kusongwa ngokwengubo,
Ube ngangentende yesandla.
Inkabi yeleqe yogaxelek' ezingcingweni.
Ayisakuba naw' amandl' okuxhentsa.
Iya kub' idukekile yidyokhwe nayipuluwa,
Sigilane ngezifuba njengezabonkol' emcepheni.
Iintombi zethu zolotyolwa ngamaqhosha,
Zintwe' eziman' ukuqhawuka zihlangana.
Kuthiwa namhl' igazi malingaphalali,
Ukuhlanganis' amathile namathile,
Ukuze singakhothani njengemaz' ikhoth' ithole,
Iqhutywa luthando nabubushushu begazi.
Linako n' iqhosh' ukukhoth' elinye?
Ew' indod' igilane nomolokazana,
Unyan' angamhlonel' uninazala,
Sisong' amadolo, singabi nak' ukunaba,
Kub' umhlab' ufinyeziwe.

The shrinking and fencing in of the land

St John Page Yako

So say the children of the Royal House,
although the land is no longer ours.
This land will be folded like a blanket,
till it is the size of the palm of a hand.
The racing ox will become enmeshed in the fencing wire.
It will no longer have the strength to dance freely.
It will be worn out by the yoke and the plough.
We will bump breast to breast like tadpoles in a calabash ladle.
The bride price of our daughters will be paid in coins –
trivial things that come and go, constantly being exchanged.
Nowadays it is said that blood should not be spilled,
one nation meeting another in conflict,
but now we no longer lick each other like a cow licks her calf,
driven by love and inborn instinct.
Can one coin lick another caringly?
A man may now bicker with his son's wife,
and a son may now forgo respecting his wife's mother!
We fold up our knees – unable to stretch out,
because the land has been shrunk.

Translated from isiXhosa by Koos Oosthuysen

Ukwenziwa komkhonzi

JJR Jolobe

Andisenakubuza ndisithi kunjani na
Ukukhanywa yintambo yedyokhwe emqaleni,
Kuba ndizibonele kwinkabi yomqokozo.
Ubumfama bamehlo busukile ndagqala,
Kuba ndikubonile ukwenziwa komkhonzi
    Kwinkatyana yedyokhwe.

Yabigudile intle, izalelw' inkululo,
Ingaceli nto mntwini, izingca ngobunkomo.
Uthe umntu mayibanjwe iqeqeshwe ithambe,
Ezilungiselela ngokunga uyasiza,
Kuba ndikubonile ukwenziwa komkhonzi
    Kwinkatyana yedyokhwe.

Inge ingamangala ikhusel' ilungelo.
Yangqingwa yabiyelwa ngobulumko namava.
Amaqhinga ooyisa kufunw' iqobozeke.
Isizathu esihle singafihla ububi,
Kuba ndikubonile ukwenziwa komkhonzi
    Kwinkatyana yedyokhwe.

Irhintyelwe ngeentambo, zayidla ebuntloko,
Yangxolizwa, yakhatywa, kwaphathwa kulelezwa.
Injongo yona inye mayithwale idyokhwe.
Lolwezulu uqeqesho olujong' umqeqeshwa,
Kuba ndikubonile ukwenziwa komkhonzi
    Kwinkatyana yedyokhwe.

The making of a slave

JJR Jolobe

I can no longer ask: how did it feel?
This strangling of the yoke cord,
because I have seen it with my own eyes in a chained ox.
Blindness left my eyes as I suddenly realised:
> I have seen the making of a slave
> in a young yoke-ox.

Glossy he was, beautiful, born to be free,
he asked nothing from anybody.
He only wanted to be proud of being a young ox,
but then somebody said, "Catch him, tame him" – as if it was to
   help him:
> I have seen the making of a slave
> in a young yoke-ox.

He strove to resist, strove to win his freedom,
he was surrounded, fenced in by schemes and plots.
They conquered him with cunning, "He has to be educated",
a harmless word but a mask for calamity:
> I have seen the making of a slave
> in a young yoke-ox.

He was bound in thongs which carved into his head,
he was whipped, kicked and occasionally stroked,
but the aim remained the same: to get the yoke on his neck.
Only the privileged were educated in their own interest:
> I have seen the making of a slave
> in a young yoke-ox.

Iqondo lokuphela, ubekiwe loo mqobo,
Yajikela nentambo entanyeni bukhanywa,
Kwathiwa igqityiwe, yofakwa emkhondweni
Ukufunda intando yomlawuli umnini-yo,
Kuba ndikubonile ukwenziwa komkhonzi
     Kwinkatyana yedyokhwe.

Ibe ngakhabalaza, izam' ukuqhawula,
Kwathethwa ngeziniya. Ijonge nangasemva
Iba iyaxakisa, koko kuthiwe: "Betha."
Obotshiwey' uyinto yokudlala kwigwala,
Kuba ndikubonile ukwenziwa komkhonzi
     Kwinkatyana yedyokhwe.

Ibe ngasadalala yalunywa emsileni.
Xa limbi ndiyibone igweba nangophondo
Kuwayo umqotyozwa wamzuzu begazi-nye.
Ubunzima bedyokhwe budal' ugxekwano,
Kuba ndikubonile ukwenziwa komkhonzi
     Kwinkatyana yedyokhwe.

Lalingathi limnyam' izulu kukhumezela.
Ndijonge elundeni, ndalibona libomvu
Kuthontsiza igazi, umkhondo woxhathiso,
Ibuzisa ikhaya, umzi wenkululeko,
Kuba ndikubonile ukwenziwa komkhonzi
     Kwinkatyana yedyokhwe.

Ime buxe kudinwa, kungekho luvelwano.
Yasitsho esikrakra isililo ibonga.
Kunyenyiswe kancinci ukuba iphefumle,
Kwabuya kwaqiniswa ibulawa umoya,

Then the last phase dawned: the yoke was on his neck,
the halter around the throat tight, almost strangling him,
but they said, "Our work is done",
from now on, with the others, he will obey the owner and master:
>I have seen the making of a slave
>in a young yoke-ox.

He kicked, tried to break out
but the whips talked.
He twisted around trying to ward them off, but they said, "Beat him!"
A slave is the plaything of a weakling:
>I have seen the making of a slave
>in a young yoke-ox.

Although he floundered and fell, he was continuously beaten at
>the tail.
At times I even saw how he gaffed
his yoke-ox partner, his friend, with his horn.
Suffering under the yoke breeds enmity between brothers:
>I have seen the making of a slave
>in a young yoke-ox.

The sky had darkened with gentle rain.
I saw his hump,
it was red with blood, the mark of revolt;
he aches for the place where he once was free:
>I have seen the making of a slave
>in a young yoke-ox.

Dead still, tired, nowhere was there any sympathy,
he bellowed bitterly, deep sounds.
The halter was loosened a little – so he could breathe

Kuba ndikubonile ukwenziwa komkhonzi
     Kwinkatyana yedyokhwe.

Ndiyibone mva seyaqobozeka yathamba,
Itsal' umbaxa-mbini wekhuba etshoniswe
Waphelela ikhonza, ikhefuza igcuma.
Ukufa kukuqhutywa, impilo kuzenzela,
Kuba ndikubonile ukwenziwa komkhonzi
     Kwinkatyana yedyokhwe.

Ndiyibone inyuka iminqantsa yomendo,
Ithwele imithwalo enzima ixelenga,
Iludaka kubila ingenisela omnye.
Incasa yomsebenzi yinxaxheba kuvuno,
Kuba ndikubonile ukwenziwa komkhonzi
     Kwinkatyana yedyokhwe.

Ndiyibon' ilambile ngaphantsi kwaloo mbuso,
Iliso liinyembezi, umxhel' ujacekile,
Ibe ingasakwazi nokuchasa imbuna.
Ithemba yimigudu ezond' inkululeko,
Kuba ndikubonile ukwenziwa komkhonzi
     Kwinkatyana yedyokhwe.

then was tightened again and he gasped for air:
> I have seen the making of a slave
> in a young yoke-ox.

I saw him later, crushed and enslaved,
pulling a double ploughshare deeply through the earth
obedient, struggling for breath, in pain – he was being driven to
  his death.
Life is to be lived for oneself:
> I have seen the making of a slave
> in a young yoke-ox.

I saw him strain against the steepest uphills
so heavily burdened it made him reel;
the mud of sweat produced a crop for another,
the taste of work his only share in the harvest:
> I have seen the making of a slave
> in a young yoke-ox.

I saw him hungry while he worked and sweated,
tears filled his eyes while his soul was destroyed,
he could resist nothing any more.
Only the idea of freedom kept him breathing in hope:
> I have seen the making of a slave
> in a young yoke-ox.

Translated from isiXhosa by Koos Oosthuysen and Antjie Krog

Umbhinqo weAfrika!

Nontsizi Mgqwetho

Ngawutsho! Ngwevu yakade enguwe.
Ngawutsho! Sidela sobuye sikholwe.
Ngawutsho! Uzeke kwakhona iindaba
Ngawutsho! Zemihla yobawo nemvaba.

Kwakunjani na ngelo xa? Ngawutsho,
Kuphekwa ngeembiza zodongwe, khe sive.
Kwakunjani na ngelo xa? Ngawutsho,
Kubhinqw' izikumba zeenkomo, masive.

Namana nilanda, nisithi: ngawutsho.
Bonisani othakathileyo, khe sive,
Xa nanibona abelungu, ngawutsho,
Becande iilwandle ngeelwandle, masive.

Mazithethe neembongi mhla kwaw' iinyembezi
Zombhinqo weAfrika. Sincede, Mhlekazi,
Owawuphilisa umphefumlo woHlanga
Lwezizw' ezintsundu ngaphantsi kwelanga.

Ezinye izizwe zihlel' ekucaceni;
Owethu umzi uhlel' ebumnyameni.
Wawa ngenyani umbhinqo weAfrika,
Safuna ukuncama, thina mzi kaNgqika.

Wawa ngenyani umbhinqo weAfrika.
KwaneBhayibhile isongwa isombuluka,
Apho zikhon' iinkosi zasemlungwini
EzineeBhayibhile ezingoombaxa-mbini.

The African waistcloth has fallen!

Nontsizi Mgqwetho

Tell us! Elder who has been around,
tell us! We underestimate until we believe,
tell us! Say more about this burning issue,
tell us! About the times of our forefathers and their wisdom.

How was it those days? Tell us!
When people cooked with clay pots – let's hear!
How was it those days? Tell us!
When people wore cow hides around their waists – let's hear!

You remember how it happened – tell us,
expose the one who bewitched us – let's hear,
when you saw white people – tell us,
they crossed seas and oceans – let's hear.

Let the iimbongi speak as well! About the days the tears fell,
of the African waistcloth, please, sir,
the waistcloth that healed the soul of the nation,
African nations under the sun.

Other nations are enlightened –
our nation dwells in darkness;
the African waistcloth has truly fallen,
and we, the house of Ngqika, began to lose hope.

The African waistcloth has truly fallen,
and the Bible is opened only to be closed.
Where the rulers are white people,
the Bible is double-tongued.

Mazithethe neembongi mhla kwaw' iinyembezi
Zombhinqo weAfrika. Sincede, Mhlekazi.
Ungumenzi weemfama uzenza ngabom.
Ngowungaqalanga ngathi ukwenza ngabom.

UloNgqina izingela imipefumlo,
Uyizingela ngabelung', asiphefumli.
UloHlanganis' imihlamb' eyalanayo,
Hlanganisa ke le yethu yalanayo.

Lathetha ixilongo lisibizile.
Nanko umbhinqo weAfrika uwile
Owawuyingubo esiyambatha thina,
UloNgubo-nkulu siyambatha thina.

Yabinza nenkwenkwezi isixelela:
Ningakhonzi izithixo, notshabalala.
Yayingumkhokeli ikhokela thina,
UloMkhokeli usikhokela thina.

UnguWena-wena uhlel' enyangweni.
Khuphani oothixo basebuginweni.
UloThixo-mkulu ngosezulwini
Odlula oombhayimbhayi basesilungwini.

UnguWena-wena, Khaka lenyaniso.
Sakuphethela ngawe, Khaka lenyaniso.
UnguWena-wena, Nqaba yenyaniso.
Kwinqaba yakho sonqaba ngenyaniso.

Le mali inkulu na sayibiza na?
Lo mzi wabo na, sawubiza na?

Let the iimbongi speak as well
about the day that the tears of the African waistcloth fell, please sir.
Help us, Lord!
You created the blind deliberately.

You should not have deliberately started with us.
You hunter of souls on a hunt,
you hunt using white people, leaving us unable to breathe;
you, the unifier of divided flocks, unite, therefore, our divided flock.

The trumpet flourish is calling us,
there it is! The African waistcloth has fallen.
That was the blanket that used to cover us,
you were the outspread blanket covering us.

And the shooting star is telling us:
you must not worship idols, you will perish;
that star was the leader who led us.
You are the leader leading us.

You are the one who dwells in heaven.
Reject the idols of the unbelievers.
You are the great God who is in heaven,
greater than the guns of the white people.

You are the one, oh Shield-of-Truth,
we shall seek protection from your shield of truth.
You are the one, oh Fortress-of-Truth,
in your fortress, we will truly take refuge.

Is this the high price He paid for us? Did we ask for it?
This house of theirs – did we ask for it?

Uwile ngabo umbhinqo wabamnyama,
Tarhu, Xhaka elimnyama kwabamnyama!

Camagu!

It has fallen! It is because of them the African waistcloth has fallen.
Have mercy, oh Black-Shield-of-the-Black-People.

It is done!

Translated from isiXhosa by Zukile Jama and Loyiso Mletshe

Moafrika

Atwell Sidwell Mopeli-Paulus

Ke khotsofetse ke seo ke leng sona,
Le hojane naha ea heso e metse tšehlo;
Moafrika re fetohile likhutsana,
Re fetohile balichaba naheng ea rōna;
Naha ea rōna e fetotsoe lehaha la masholu.

Teng ho phela ba mefuta-futa eohle,
Batho ba hlokang ho hauhela Moafrika,
Ba ikemiselitseng ho ripitlela Afrika;
Kajeno ba ipona borena ka nah'a Moafrika.
Moafrika, tsoha, naha e hapiloe ke balichaba.

Letsatsi ho chaba ha lona, ka mehla
Ho rōna ho tlisa ho hlora ha meea:
Ka mehla re ipotsa lipotso tsena:
Na le 'na ke tla finyella mola?
Ke'ng ha 'mala oa ka o mphetohetse?
'Na ke tšoana le koekoe ea morao!

Ka lilemo le lilemo, ho fihlellana,
Ke b'esale ke kolla ntsi hanong;
Tlhalefo ea ka ha e na molemo ho 'na,
Ka lilemo ke fetohile mo-kōma-lerōle,
Esita le tseo e leng litoka ho 'na.

Mohlomong mali-mabe a 'maleng oa me,
Oona e leng sesomo ho balichaba;
'Mala oa ka o tšoana le naha ea ka,
Afrika ke naha ea mobu oa seloko;
Monongoaha le eona seli le tla e chabela.

An African

Atwell Sidwell Mopeli-Paulus

I am satisfied with what I am,
although our land has grown devil's thorns;
we Africans have become orphans,
we have become foreigners in our own country;
our country has been turned into a cave of thieves.

Here live all the different races,
people who do not have any feeling for an African,
who are all out to shatter Africa,
who regard themselves today as kings in the country of Africans.
African, wake up – the country has been seized by foreigners.

The rising of our daily sun
brings loneliness to our souls;
daily we ask ourselves these questions:
Shall I ever arrive in freedom?
Why has my colour turned against me?
I am like the quail flying up last.

Year after year, one following the other,
I have to take flies from my hungry mouth;
my wisdom has brought me nothing,
for years, I have been nothing but a dust-eater,
even in things that are mine by right.

Perhaps the curse lies in my skin,
my skin is derided among foreigners;
my skin is the colour of my country –
African child of the loamy black soil,
for you also, the sun will rise.

Moafrika, ngoan'a mobu oa seloko,
Ngoan'a tsoaletsoeng naheng ea lefifi;
Le eena letsatsi le tla mo chabela,
Tsa monene li tla fetoha mouoane,
Le 'na ke Moafrika, ngoan'a nah'a Afrika.

African, child of this black earth,
child born in this black land;
also for you, light will dawn,
the past will be like morning mist;
also me, I am an African, child of Africa.

Translated from Sesotho by Johannes Lenake

Dingana le Maburu

LD Raditladi

Lefatshe le le ne le apere mebala,
Le tlhanotse dikobo tsa letlhafula.
Legae la Kgosi le ne le sa tsofala,
La bo le dutse godimo ga lekhujana,
Kwa tlase molapo o epile lefatshe,
O goaletse ka metsi a masetlha o kgotshe,
O tlhaphoga tlhe jaaka mabele a motshe,
O duduetswa ke digogwane serena.

Letsatsi le ne le wetse bodikelo,
Marang a galaletsa lesenamelo,
A tlhakana le lesedi la molelo
Gobo la ngwedi le ne le le lenene.
Dingana le Maburu ba itshegela fela,
Ba bua dikgang tsa bone ba di tlopela,
Tsa thamaga di rutlarutla megala,
Tsa dipitse badisa ba sa di bone.

Mophato wa Kgosing o no o itshomotse
Ka dikola o bina ka thata, moletse,
O tlola fa le fale jaaka letsetse,
Maoto a tsholeletsega le kwa godimo
A bata lefatshe gararo moribe,
Ditlhogo di ntse di kobile dibebe,
Dihuba tsa bone di apere dithebe,
Thobane di duma le phefo godimo.

Ditlhobolo di ne di adile matlhaku,
Di nyakgatha fela di ntshitse boroku

Dingane and the Boers

LD Raditladi

The earth was clothed in many colours,
it shook out its spring blankets.
The king's house was well-maintained,
it sat on top of a small ridge;
below, the river ploughed a path in the earth,
it exulted in an abundance of yellow-brown water,
it used its pestle to separate the wheat from the chaff;
the frogs in it ululated like illiterate lords.

The sun had set in the west,
rays of light broke through the lattice work of the rafters,
merging with the light of the fire
because the moonlight was not enough.
Dingane and the Boers were laughing in this light,
they were discussing business and boasting
of cattle pulling ropes in a tug of war,
of horses that even herders couldn't find.

The royal regiment was then detached
and they danced better than ever before.
Look at those legs, jumping here and there light-footed like fleas,
their feet lifted high,
stamping the ground three times,
they all looked down,
their chests covered with shields,
they swung their sticks high in the wind.

The guns hung spread-out from the reed fence,
the gleaming butts clustered like aphids against the walls,

Jaaka matlhaka fela a obotswe dimeku,
Ka mosidi wa tsone ba ne ba sa o laela.
Kgara tse dintsho tse di masana a thata
Tsa latlhela ditau setlhareng se thata,
Tsa di tsenya lofatlheng lo mitlwa e thata,
Mme tsa leta sekao sa Kgosi go laila.

Molomo wa ga Kgosi Dingana wa duma,
Lentswe la Morena la utlwala bokima,
La dumisa mometso le kgodukoma,
La ratha la re: "Bulala abathakathi!"
Mephato ya Kgosi ya duma ka dikodu,
Ya rema thata ga feta bohibidu,
Madi a rotha jaaka matute le kgodu,
A konkonyega mmogo fela le mathe.

Ga Modimo re ka bo re go lemoga,
Ba boDingana re ka bo re ba tlhoboga,
Ka boDingana bo tletsetletse le naga.
Modirwa tota kana o ka lebala jang?
Motho yo o solofelang seo ruri ke mang?
A motho yoo ke Mothosa kana ke mang?
Modimo borukutlhi ga o bo itshwarele.

the barrels like peeled sugar cane reeds:
they were not loaded with gunpowder.
Then the black chests became very hard
as hard as lions being thrown into the trees,
as hard as if they were thrusting their chests into the thorns,
waiting for the King's command to devour.

The mouth of King Dingane boomed,
the King's heavy voice could be clearly heard,
the larynx and vocal chords roared,
they cut the air, "Kill the witches!"
The King's regiments roared back,
they hacked hard, until redness ran,
blood spilled thickly like sediment,
and fused freely with saliva.

If we could only follow what God says,
we would have given up on the Dinganes,
because the land is full of Dinganes.
How can a victim simply forget?
Who is it that expects that?
Is it a Xhosa or is it someone else?
God does not forgive conspiracies.

Translated from Setswana by Tšepiso Samuel Mothibi and Antjie Krog

Ntoa ea Jeremane (1914)

BM Khaketla

Hloaea tsebe u mamele oa nkhono,
U mamele masisimosa-'mele:
Taba tsa banna li mosenekeng,
Li batla ho reetsoa ka tsebe-lethoethoe.

E n'e le ka khoeli ea Phato, selemo,
Meea, Lesotho, e foka, e puputla,
Ho thunya marōle a mafubelu tlere!
Kahohle ho utloahala lepukupuku.

Ra utloa ho hlajoa mokhosi ka mose,
Ka mose ho maoatle ho la Jiropo,
Ho beheloa chaba tsa lohle lefatše
Bosōtō ba chaba tsa nah'a Jiropo.

Ke ofe ea sa ka a utloa molumo?
Molumo oa lithunya le oa likanono?
Lerata la tsona la thiba litsèbè,
La tšela maoatle la fihla Lesotho.

Mosotho a botsa: "Molato ke ofe,
Ha ho ruthuthanoa, ho lla likanono?"
Ba mo oeoeletsa, ba bua moeka:
Lipoho lia koeba, li fata makoatsi!

"Ke ea Jeremane le ea Engelane,
Li khonya haholo, li bohla senare;
Ho khonya ha tsona ho khoesa maseea,
Lebese le hlanye le le matsoeleng!"

The war with Germany (1914)

BM Khaketla

Sharpen your ears, child of Grandma,
and listen to a story that makes the body tremble with concern:
matters of men are at a bottleneck,
and need to be listened to with a keen ear.

It was in the month of August, already spring,
the time in Lesotho when the winds blow strongly,
shooting up dusts of crimson!
From every direction, the wind was flapping up a plethora of dust.

That was the time we heard a piercing alarm from overseas,
from far away, in the land of Europe,
reporting to all the nations of the world
the misery of the nations of Europe.

Was there anyone there who did not hear that thunder,
the thunder of guns and cannons?
Their din deafened the ears,
it crossed oceans and reached Lesotho.

Then a Mosotho asked, "What is the reason
for this barrage, and the wall-breaking sound of cannons?"
The truth was shouted at him,
"The bulls are goring, they throw up the dust that they tear from
    the ground!

"It is the bulls of Germany and of England,
they roar terribly, they bellow like buffaloes;
their bellowing makes infants pull away from the nipple,
and curdles the milk that is still in mothers' breasts.

Oa Botšelela, moroala-korone,
E n'e le koloane le benya sekama;
A hana ho utloa, a tela borena,
Mophato oa hae a o khobokanya.

A loana senna le thaka tsa hae,
Likulo tsa hae leholiotsoana,
Tsa tsosa lifefo, tsa chesa linaha,
Tsa ba tsa tlabola K'heisare litelu.

Na o n'a ka khutsa mor'a Lerotholi,
Setlōlō sa Kholu le sa Fitoria?
A hana hehehe, a latola bosehla,
A bolela: eabo ha e che a le teng.

A tea mololi likhoari tsa utloa,
Ha tlōla maqhaoe le liqhoqhobela,
Ha tlōla mehohla e telu li thata,
Ha tlōl'a sebele malala-a-laotsoe.

Maseea a e-khoa a siea matsoele,
A khoesoa ke oa e moholo, mololi,
Morena Kerefese oa Lerotholi,
A mathela mose ho thiba semeche.

"Bathusi ba lōna ke Majeremane,"
Ho bua lithoto le litseketseke;
"Le a rapelle a pshatle mahata
A Manyesemane, balotsanahali!"

Ba bang ba bua, ba pepesa feela;
"Satane oa khale hase le molemo,

The Sixth George that Bore the Crown,
still smeared with the glittering antimony of the initiate,
refused to listen and instead put his kingship on the line.
He gathered his regiment.

He and his peers fought like men,
their bullets a tornado,
they raised storms, they scorched lands,
they even singed the Kaiser's beard.

Could the son of Lerotholi then keep quiet,
last black grandson of Kholu and Victoria?
No, no, no, he refused the colour of yellow neutrality,
and declared, "The king's home will not burn down while I am
    here."

He whistled because partridges call one another with the
    gwarrie call that they recognise.
Up jumped the gallant heroes and the valiant,
up jumped the strong with hard beards,
up jumped those who were ready to begin battle today although
    they heard about it only yesterday.

Infants weaned and abandoned the breast,
they were weaned by the Old One's whistle,
King Griffiths of Lerotholi,
he hastened overseas to halt the colliding smash.

"Your saviours are the Germans,"
said the fools and the idiots.
"Pray that they crunch the skulls
of the great conniving English!"

E mocha, kamehla, hase ho chesaka!
Rōna re rata oa rōna oa khale."

Ho joang kajeno? E timile hlaha.
Ea tingoa ka eng? Ka mali a Basotho.
Tšepiso li kae tsa bolokolohi?
U tsebe, ngoan'eso, setsoeng ho hōle!

Some said, opening up the real issue:
"The Satan of old may be better
than the new one, always burning, without rest!
We prefer the old one."

How are things today? The blaze has been stamped out.
What was it extinguished with? Basotho blood.
Where are those promises of freedom now?
You know, my brothers and sisters, it is too difficult to bite your
    own elbow!

Translated from Sesotho by Tšepiso Samuel Mothibi

Ukutshona kukaMendi

SEK Mqhayi

Ewe, le nto kakade yinto yaloo nto!
Thina, nto zaziyo, asothukanga nto.
Sibona kamhlope, sithi bekumelwe;
Sitheth' engqondweni, sithi kufanelwe;
Xa bekungenjalo, bekungayi kulunga.
Ngoko ke, Sotase, kwaqal' ukulunga!
Le nqanaw' uMendi namhlanje yendisile,
Nal' igazi lethu lisikhonzisile!

Asinithumanga ngazo izicengo;
Asinithenganga ngayo imibengo.
Bekungenganzuzo zimakhwezi-khwezi;
Bekungengandyebo zingangeenkwenkwezi.
Sikwatsho nakuni, bafel' eAfrika,
KwelaseJamani yasempumalanga
NelaseJamani yasentshonalanga.
Bekungembek' eninayo kuKumkani;
Bekungentobeko yenu kwiBritani.

Mhla nashiy' ikhaya sithethile nani;
Mhla nashiy' iintsapho salathile kuni,
Mhla sabamb' izandla, mhla kwamanz' amehlo.
Mhla balil' oonyoko, bangqukrulek' ooyihlo,
Mhla nazishiy' ezi ntaba zakowenu,
Nayinikel' imiv' imilamb' ezwe lenu,
Asitshongo na kuni, midak' akowethu,
Ukuthi: "Kwelo zwe nilidini lethu"?
Ngesibinge ngantoni na ke kade?
Idini lomzi liyintoni na kade?

Sinking of the Mendi

SEK Mqhayi

Yes, this is the way things happen, after all.
We who are in the know were not surprised.
We see clearly, it was inevitable.
In our minds, we say it is fitting that it happened.
If it did not happen, things would not have returned to their
    proper order.
Therefore, Sotase, things began to be right.
That ship, Mendi, today is in the deep,
and our blood suffered the ultimate sacrifice.

We did not bribe you with appeals.
We did not entice you with titbits of meat.
It was not for gain that we glittered like stars.
It was not for gain as prolific as the stars.
We also say to you who died in Africa,
in Germany of the sunrise
and in Germany of the sunset,
it was not because of an honour bestowed by the king,
it was not because of your loyalty toward Britain.

The day you left home, we spoke to you;
the day you left your family, we addressed you;
the day we held your hand, the day our eyes watered;
the day the mothers lamented and the fathers cried under their
    breath;
the day you left our mountains,
when the rivers of our country lay behind you,
didn't we address you, the people of our country, saying,
"In that country, you are our sacrifice"?

Asingamathol' amaduna omzi na?
Asizizithandwa zesizwe kade na?

Ngoku kuthetha ke siyendelisela,
Sibekis' ezantsi, sihlahla indlela.
AsinguHabeli na idini lomhlaba?
AsinguMesiya na elasezulwini?

Thuthuzelekani ngoko, zinkedama;
Thuthuzelekani ngoko, bafazana.
Kuf' omnye kakade, mini kwakhiw' omnye;
Kukhonza mnye kade, ze kuphil' abanye.
Ngala mazwi sithi thuthuzelekani;
Ngokwenjenje kwethu sithi, yakhekani.
Lithatheni eli qhalo labadala,
Kuba bathi: "Akuhlanga lungehlanga!"

Awu! Zaf' iint' ezinkulu zeAfrika.
Isindiwe le nqanawa yada yazika,
Kwaf' amakhalipha, amafa-nankosi
Agazi lithetha kwiNkosi yeenkosi.
Ukufa kwawo kunomvuzo nomvuka.
Ndinga ndingema nawo ngomhla wokuvuka,
Ndingqambe njengomnye osebenzileyo;
Ndikhanye nje ngomso oqaqambileyo.
        Makube njalo!

What else could we have offered as a sacrifice?
The sacrifice of a house, what is it after all?
Is it not the male calves of the homestead?
Is it not the beloved ones of the nation?

Now, we remember the sinking to the deep;
now we recall the path to the bottom.
Is Abel not the sacrifice of the earth?
Is the Messiah not the one of heaven?

Be comforted then, you orphans.
Be comforted then, you young women.
One dies, so another may flourish.
One serves, so another may prosper.
With these words, be consoled, we say.
In saying this, we say, be restored.
Accept this proverb from the old people.
They say, "It does not happen without happening."

Oh no! The great sons of Africa have died!
This boat survived till it sank.
The brave heroes have died, sacrificing themselves for their king.
Their blood speaks to the King of kings.
One day, their loss will be atoned for.
Oh, I long to stand with them on the Day of Resurrection
where I will achieve a glorious radiance
and will shine like a brilliant morning.
    Let it be so!

Translated from isiXhosa by Koos Oosthuysen and Gabeba Baderoon

Ukutshona kukaMendi

SEK Mqhayi

Ewe, le nto kakade yinto yaloo nto!
Thina, nto zaziyo, asothukanga nto.
Sibona kamhlope, sithi bekumelwe;
Sitheth' engqondweni, sithi kufanelwe;
Xa bekungenjalo, bekungayi kulunga.
Ngoko ke, Sotase, kwaqal' ukulunga!
Le nqanaw' uMendi namhlanje yendisile,
Nal' igazi lethu lisikhonzisile!

Asinithumanga ngazo izicengo;
Asinithenganga ngayo imibengo.
Bekungenganzuzo zimakhwezi-khwezi;
Bekungengandyebo zingangeenkwenkwezi.
Sikwatsho nakuni, bafel' eAfrika,
KwelaseJamani yasempumalanga
NelaseJamani yasentshonalanga.
Bekungembek' eninayo kuKumkani;
Bekungentobeko yenu kwiBritani.

Mhla nashiy' ikhaya sithethile nani;
Mhla nashiy' iintsapho salathile kuni,
Mhla sabamb' izandla, mhla kwamanz' amehlo.
Mhla balil' oonyoko, bangqukrulek' ooyihlo,
Mhla nazishiy' ezi ntaba zakowenu,
Nayinikel' imiv' imilamb' ezwe lenu,
Asitshongo na kuni, midak' akowethu,
Ukuthi: "Kwelo zwe nilidini lethu"?
Ngesibinge ngantoni na ke kade?
Idini lomzi liyintoni na kade?

The sinking of the Mendi

SEK Mqhayi

Ewe! This is what it is!
We, the ones with premonition, are not shocked.
We see clearly, and say it was expected;
We say to ourselves: it is coming;
If it wasn't like that, nothing would be right.
Therefore, Sotase! It was the beginning of righteousness!
Today this ship, Mendi, has united various races,
and our blood has made us serve!

We did not have to beg you;
we did not buy you with pieces of meat;
we did not have to give you precious things;
we did not have to promise you a plenteous harvest –
we are saying this even to you who died in Africa,
or in the sunrise side of Germany –
or in the sunset side of Germany –
you went because of your respect for your own king,
you went because you accepted your shared humanity with Britain.

The day you left home, we spoke to you,
the day you left your families, we pointed you out,
the day we shook hands, our eyes became wet,
the day your mothers cried, your fathers sobbed,
the day you left these mountains of your home,
and left behind the rivers of your country,
didn't we say to you, our brothers,
"In that country you are our sacrifice for freedom"?
What else could we have rendered to our ancestors?
What is the sacrifice of a home?

Asingamathol' amaduna omzi na?
Asizizithandwa zesizwe kade na?

Ngoku kuthetha ke siyendelisela,
Sibekis' ezantsi, sihlahla indlela.
AsinguHabeli na idini lomhlaba?
AsinguMesiya na elasezulwini?

Thuthuzelekani ngoko, zinkedama;
Thuthuzelekani ngoko, bafazana.
Kuf' omnye kakade, mini kwakhiw' omnye;
Kukhonza mnye kade, ze kuphil' abanye.
Ngala mazwi sithi thuthuzelekani;
Ngokwenjenje kwethu sithi, yakhekani.
Lithatheni eli qhalo labadala,
Kuba bathi: "Akuhlanga lungehlanga!"

Awu! Zaf' iint' ezinkulu zeAfrika.
Isindiwe le nqanawa yada yazika,
Kwaf' amakhalipha, amafa-nankosi
Agazi lithetha kwiNkosi yeenkosi.
Ukufa kwawo kunomvuzo nomvuka.
Ndinga ndingema nawo ngomhla wokuvuka,
Ndingqambe njengomnye osebenzileyo;
Ndikhanye nje ngomso oqaqambileyo.
     Makube njalo!

Is it not the male calves of the household?
Is it not those who are loved by the nation?

With these words we are grounding ourselves,
we are sinking, we are paving the way.
Is Abel not the sacrifice of earth?
Is the Messiah not the one for heaven?

Be consoled, orphans,
be consoled then, young wives.
The truth is that one dies when one is created;
the truth is one must serve, for others to be free.
By these words we pay our condolences to you,
by doing this, we say, be strong;
take the saying of the elders,
who say, "Nothing out of the ordinary has happened!"

Oh! Honourable men of Africa are dying!
The situation becomes too heavy so it sinks,
courageous men die, die together with their chief;
whose blood is recognised by the Almighty.
Something good is rising with their death;
I long to stand with them on the day of resurrection,
and shine gloriously as one who has done something good,
and shine like the first red of a glorious tomorrow.
　　Let it be!

Translated from isiXhosa by Thokozile Mabeqa and Ncedile Saule

Go nwela ga Mendi

MS Kitchin

A ga ea re mokgosi o dule moseja ole,
Go le thata, tau tse ditona di lotlhaganye;
Go le thata ya lentswe, ka banna ba sa robale,
Go bifile, ka ditlhaka di tshelepaganye,
Ga bolola mophato wa Mautlwakgosi mono.

Koloi ya metse, Mendi, e sa le e hulara
E paoganya ka bone mawatle a magolo;
E phekile malatsi, ba gopotse ntlheng ya Fora
(Le ene Fora o buiwang ga baa mmona ka matlho);
Golo ba go ileng go itse tlhapi tsa madiba.

He bagaetsho! Lalang ka ntho madi a tshologa,
Le pelo di gamuketse botlhoko di tlaa fola.
Ba ile barwa-rra-rona, ga ba na go menoga,
Bajelwe ke tau e sa sisimogeng motho mmala,
Ba meditswe ke metse a se nang pelotlhomogi.

Go no go sa bolola legatlapa lepe nabo,
Go no go ile bomorwa-loso-lo-dirwang fela –
Banna ba tswang mogang thamo ya phala e hubitse,
Banna ba tshwantshitseng bolalome le dibatana,
Thaka tse dikgolo tse di pelo di ritibetseng.

Fa mongwe a ne a ba tlhaselela lonyatsong
A re ke bodišaše ba ka mo tshoga seemo,
O ne a tlaa thanya fela lomapo lo le tsebeng
Mme fa le ene gongwe e le mosimane wa pholo,
Bogolo go ne go ka ša logong ga sala molora.

The drowning of the Mendi

MS Kitchin

We received the terrible news from over there,
it was difficult: the big lions clashed;
a cacophony of voices: men could not sleep,
a time of fury: there was no peace,
then a regiment of men loyal to the King left this place.

Mendi, the great truck of the sea, then turned its back on the land,
spearing the wild seas with men on board;
piercing the long, long way to France
(indeed, they never saw the yearned-for France with their eyes).
Where they went only the big fish of the deep knew.

My countrymen! Try to sleep even though your wound is
    seeping blood,
your hearts wrenching with pain shall heal.
They are gone, our brothers, they will never return,
they were eaten by the lion who eats everyone,
they were swallowed by waters that know no mercy.

There was no coward travelling among them,
only those who did not fear death answered the call –
men who went out when the whistle was blown,
men who were cunning like man-eaters and predatory beasts,
a group of young men with brave, serene hearts.

If anyone wants to look down on them
or try to claim they were cowards, he will regret his actions:
he will instantly lose an ear.
If he were brave enough for war,
then he would be burnt to ashes.

Mephato e boile, bone ba sa tlhokafala
Re saletse go oketsa diphatla ka diatla fela.
Bana ba Mautlwakgosi ba setse masiela,
Le magae a bone a fetogile matlotla,
Masalela a bone a tlaa tswa mpeng tsa ditlhapi.

Go no go sa bolola ope yo boboi le bone,
Go no go ile banna ba ba sa tshabeng loso:
Banna ba ba tswang mogang go le thata,
Banna ba ba ne ba tshwana le dibatana ka bogale,
Thaka tse di ne di sa tlalelwe-tlalelwe fela.

The other regiments came back, the soldiers who had not died,
we were left shading our eyes, looking for those who had not
   returned.
The children of men loyal to the King became orphans,
even their homes became dilapidated and dark,
only the big fish of the deep could release their bones.

There was no coward travelling among them,
there were only those who do not fear death:
the kind of men who emerge only in troubled times,
men whose fury was like that of predatory beasts,
young men who could not be rattled or shaken.

Translated from Setswana by Stephen Masote,
David wa Maahlamela and Tšepiso Samuel Mothibi

A! Silimela!

SEK Mqhayi

A! Silimela!
AmaNdlamb' amatsha,
Hay' amaNdlamb' amatsha!
Inkos' am ngumntakaNdluzodaka.
Yindod' ezalwa ngabantw' ababini;
Izalwa nguMakinana noNopasi.
UNopasi yintombi kaMon' umhlophe kaNtshunqe,
Umhlophe kaNtshunqe kwaBomvana.
NguLuhad' igama lakhe,
Umbambo zemka zabuyelela.
Ngaphantsi kwelitye kuyoyikeka,
Kuba zilaph' iinzwana namadikazi.
Ngubani n' ongevanga?
Ngubani n' ongevang' ukuba sithwasil' isilimela kwaNdlambe?
Isilimela ke yinkwenkwez' enkulu yakwaPhalo.

Incwadi yaphum' eGqolongc' ivela kuLayithi noTshalisi.
Yawel' iNciba, yawel' uMbhashe,
Kwal' uk'b' ifik' eMgazana yathetha,
Yathi: "Goduka, Makinan', ufil' uyihlo.
Ufel' eMthuman' emazants' eQangqalala.
Goduk' uye kubus' amaNdlamb', akanamntu."
Wath' uMakinana: "Ndiyeza, ndisavun' amazimba."
Wath' esitsho wab' eyifak' eyakowabo yakuloNkanti,
Wankqenkqeza phambil' uNtakamhlophe,
Wath' uk'ba abesek'ngeneni kweTyityaba, yafik' incwadi kaFen',
    isithi:
"Buya, Makinan', ilizwe selonakele."
Wath' uMakinana: "Hayi, asilisiko lakoweth' ukubuya ngomva."

A! Silimela! Hail! Oh, Pleiades!

SEK Mqhayi

A! Silimela! Hail! Oh, Pleiades!
The young amaNdlambe!
Yes, the young amaNdlambe!
Hey! My chief's the descendant of Ndluzodaka.
He is a man born of two people.
He was brought into the world by Makinana and Nopasi.
Nopasi is the daughter of Mona the light-skinned one of Ntshunqe,
the fair son of Ntshunqe in Bomvanaland.
His name is Luhadi.
A rib who was ripped out and came back.
Under the stone it is dreadful,
because that is where the handsome men and women are.
Who has not heard?
Who has not heard that the Pleiades have risen at the place of
    Ndlambe?
Now the Pleiades is the major star of the land of Phalo.

A letter went forth from Gqolongco, coming from Layithi and
    Charles.
It crossed the Kei river and crossed the Mbashe,
but before it reached the Mgazana river, it spoke
and said, "Go home, Makinana, your father has died.
He died at Mthumana, below Qangqalala.
Come home and guide the amaNdlambe – they have no one."
Then Makinana said, "I am coming, but I'm still harvesting the
    sorghum."
Saying this, he tendered his own letter from Nkanti's home.
He forged ahead, this child of the light-skinned one, continuing
    his journey.

Wath' esitsho wab' etyhudis' ejonge phambili.

Uth' ak'ba seMpethu wafik' uFeni ngesiqu, wathi: "Ndithi,

Ndithi buya, Makinana, uza nerhola."

Wath' uMakinana: "Hayi,

Asilisiko lakoweth' ukubuya ngomva."

Kwalil' uk'b' abeseDrayibhoso

Yavel' eyakwaNtsasan' ityeth' iintong' ezinkone.

Kulapho yaqala khon' ukugagana.

Yatshay' impampile yaseMlungwini;

Yatshay' impampile yasemaXhoseni.

Yaw' imikhuthuk' amacal' omabini.

Yarhox' ekaNtsasana, yasinga kwaseQumrha.

Wee tyuu uNdluzodaka,

Waya kutsho kuNdanda kooVece kuXesimagqagala.

Bizan' izizwe, kuza kwabiw' iinkwenkwezi.

Iinkwenkwezi mazabiwe.

Nina beSuthu, thathan' uCanzibe.

Niya kwabelana nabeTshwana nabaTshopi,

Nazo zonk' eziny' iintlang' ezinezishuba.

Nina bakwaZulu, thathan' amaKroza.

Niya kwabelana namaSwazi namaTshopi namaTshangana,

Neziny' iintlang' ezingamajarha.

Nina baseBritani, thathan' iKhwezi.

Niya kubambana namaJamani namaBhulu,

Noko nibantu bangakwaziy' ukwabelana,

Nisuke nenz' imfazwe yamaBhulu neyamaJamani.

Siza kubambana ngeSilimela thina mabandla kaPhalo,

Yona nkwenkwez' inkulu,

Kuba yinkwenkwezi yokubal' iminyaka,

Yokubal' iminyaka yobudoda,

When he reached the Tyityaba, a letter came from Feni, saying,
"Come back, Makinana, the country is in disarray."
And Makinana said, "No, it is not the tradition of our people to
    turn back."
Saying this, he strove ahead.
When he arrived at Mpethu, Feni himself arrived, and said,
"Come back, Makinana, with your delegation."
But Makinana said, "No!
It's not the tradition of our people to turn back."
But when they reached Draaibos,
the one from Ntsasana arrived, carrying battle-scarred weapons.
And that is where the strife began.
When the impact of the report from the side of the whites was felt,
countered by the report from Xhosaland,
everything was unclear on both sides,
and those of Ntsasana drew back and went toward Komga.
Acting quickly, Ndluzodaka went
to Ndanda at the place of the Veces with Ngqika.

Call the nations, the stars are going to be shared among them.
The stars must be handed out among the nations.
You, Basothos, take the Evening Star,
and share it with the Tswana and the Tshopi,
and all the nations that wear loincloths.
You of KwaZulu, take Orion
and share it with the Swazis, the Tshopi and the Shangaans,
and the other scattered nations.
You of Britain, take the Morning Star,
you will hold hands with the Germans and the Afrikaners,
although you are people who do not know how to share.
And so you will make war with the Afrikaners and the Germans.

Yokubal' iminyaka yobudoda,
Iminyaka yobudoda.
Ncincilili!

We, this divided house of Phalo, now is the time to share the
   Pleiades,
the most prominent of all constellations,
because it is the star of counting the years,
counting the years of manhood,
counting the years of manhood.
Yes, indeed, the years of manhood.
I fade away!

Translated from isiXhosa by Koos Oosthuysen and Gabeba Baderoon

Ingxoxo yomginwa kumagqoboka!

Nontsizi Mgqwetho

Ziph' iintombi zenu? lzwi liyintoni?
    Zigqibe lo mhlaba, zifuna ukwenda.
Ziqeshe zindlwana zishweshwe uthuli.
    Zibeth' oonomtatsi kwaThulandivile!

Oonina balila amehlo azidudu
    Kushiywa lusapo lumka bekhangele,
Beyala belila bengenakuviwa
    Zintombi zemfundo noonyana bemfundo!

Kuzel' intolongo, kwaphuk' ihovizi
    Ngala matshivela asezikolweni.
Iisertifiketi zasesimnareni
    Ziyinto yentsini ebukwa ziiJaji.

Onk' amabhedengu asezikolweni;
    Onke namasela asezikolweni;
Onke namagqwirha asezikolweni.
    Ningabokusikwa ndifung' uNontsizi.

Nikho ngakuThixo nasebuqabeni;
    Nigqobok' emini, kuhlwe niziingcuka.
Udlul' umfundisi angakubulisi,
    Kodwa ngumalusi weemvu zikaThixo.

Sothini na thina xa besenjenjalo?
    Sibambe liphi na kulo mpambapamba?
Nekratshi likuni, nina magqoboka.
    Nambathis' uThixo ngengubo yengwenya.

A resister's reply to a Christian convert!

Nontsizi Mgqwetho

Where are your daughters? What is their message?
They are all over the land looking for someone to marry,
renting and sharing dusty shacks,
dancing seductively at Thulandivile's!

Their swollen-eyed mothers weep,
their children perishing right in front of them,
admonishing, crying without being heard
by their learned sons and daughters!

Prisons are full, and offices break down
because of these educated good-for-nothings.
The certificates from the colleges
are a laughing stock when scrutinised by the judges.

All the liars are in the institutions of learning,
all the thieves are at school,
everyone, even the witches and wizards, are at school.
You must all be thrown out, I swear by Nontsizi.

You are on God's side, but also on the side of the Red-Ochred
    People.
In the daytime you are Christian converts, when it is dark you are
    wolves.
As you pass, not even the preacher greets you,
though he is the shepherd of God's flocks.

What can we do when they do that?
What should we hold onto in this confusion?

Nina magqoboka, ningoodludla nazo.
    Nayek' izikhakha, nanxib' ezomlungu.
Nithe nzwi nendlebe butywala bomlungu,
    Kodwa yen' umlungu akabudl' obenu.

Ngeemini zecawe nihamba ezindle,
    Nikhaba ibhola kunye netenise,
Nigqishel' ububi ngeZwi likaThixo,
    Nixak' uSatana usinkwabalala.

Aninaluthando, aninayo nani,
    Kodwa nizibiza ngoThixo wothando.
Loo nkolwana yenu yokusikhohlisa
    Mina ingangam ndiguqe ngedolo.

Nakufika kuthi, thina bomaqaba,
    Thina sakunoja, sithi niyinyama.
Anditsho ukuthi iZwi likaThixo
    Ukuthetha kwalo akunanyaniso.

    Camagu!

Pride reigns within you, Christian converts,
you clothe God with the garment of a crocodile.

You Christian converts are just empty followers,
you discarded your traditional garments for western clothing,
you are infatuated with the drink of the white people,
but white people never taste your traditional drink.

On worship days, you hang around on open fields,
playing football and tennis,
hiding deceitfully behind God's word.
You even amaze Satan.

You have no love, you have absolutely nothing,
yet you identify yourselves with God's love,
this little bit of faith of yours confuses us,
it is the same height as me kneeling down.

When you arrive at this place, we, the Red-Ochred People,
will roast you as we do meat.
I do not say that God's word
is devoid of truth.

  It is done!

Translated from isiXhosa by Zukile Jama and Loyiso Mletshe

Ntwa ya 1939–45

LD Raditladi

Go kile ga tsoga leruuruu maloba,
Leruuruu la marumo le dikanono,
Bana ba Yuropa ba ipetsa dihuba,
Komano ya bone ya utlwala le kwano:
Ba re, lefatshe leno ope ga a na le sema
Banna ba Yuropa botlhe ba a le lema.

Majeremane ba tswa modutla wa kgetse,
Ba itshema maruarua ba kometsa batho,
Le Mapolare ba ba meletsa metse,
Le kwa Austria le gone ba phura batho,
Merafe ya etsa diphologolo sekgweng
Di utlwile lerumo la batsomi nageng.

Bana ba thebe e setsibasehibidu,
Sesweu, setala, se motshe wa godimo,
Ba ara, bana ba motlhaba o o morodu,
Ba duma, ba etsa tladi ya legodimo:
Lentswe la bone la utlwala kwa Amerika,
Le rona ra le utlwa re le mono Aferika.

Majeremane ba rutla kwa Dankeke,
Marumo a bone a atlolola lenaga,
A thuba matlo a mantsi le dikereke;
Batho ba aga mesimeng ba se dinoga,
Fa nonyane tsa baba di kala marung,
Di latlha mae a tsone bogorogorong.

The war of 1939–45

LD Raditladi

Once upon a time thundering erupted,
a thundering of spears and cannons,
children of Europe drummed their breasts,
and their quarrel was heard here as well;
they said: no man created this world on his own,
all men of Europe ploughed it.

The Germans turned themselves into an enormous maw,
like a huge whale, they swallowed other nations:
they swallowed the villages of the Poles,
in Austria, they ground the people down.
Nations panicked like animals in the veld,
terrorised by gunfire in the dense bushes.

Children with ochre-coloured shields,
with white, green and sky-blue colours,
they thundered, these children of the red soil,
they roared like the lightning of the sky:
their disputes were heard far away in America;
in Africa, we also heard them.

The Germans wrenched out Dunkirk,
their spears reached all over,
destroying many homes and churches,
while people dwelt underground even though they were not
    snakes,
when birds of the enemy roofed the sky,
dropping their eggs into space.

Kwa Fora Mafora ba relela, ba wa,
Rona Maaferika mme ra ema matseba,
Kgodumo tsa leselesele go lowa.
Morafe wa mokgophana wa motlhaba,
Ra ema fela, sesweu senyesemane,
Ra ema sesole, bana ba basimane.

Ditlhobolo ra di rwala mo magetleng,
Le bo-"Quick march", ra ba gata re sa ba itse,
"Present arms", tlhobolo ra e baa mo diphatleng.
"Attention", ra mo ema sekgomo a letsetse;
Ra phunya mafatshe ra fitlha Egepeto,
Benkasi ra mo tsena re le mophato.

Tse dintshontsho tsa matutu re mabeta,
Re betabetanye le Mantariana,
Difofane tsa bone ra utlwa di feta,
Di lelekilwe ke matshubametsana,
A pagololang di godimo di fofa,
O bone di latlha diphuka di lefa.

Hitlara re kile ra utlwa a ipolela,
A re tladi e kileng ya tshosa ditšhaba,
Le basadi ya ba tlholela go lela.
Rona ra re, phenyo ka matlho o tla e leba,
Ka diatla yone gone ga a na go e tshwara:
MaJeremane ba roroma diphara!

Lerumo la rona matlhakanyabatho,
Le tlhakantse Mosoleni le Japane,
La etsa dinare la robakanya batho,
Hitlara la mo gadika jaaka phane,

In France, the French slipped and fell,
but we Africans stood alert,
like Kgodumo-monsters of the thorn trees ready to fight.
We were dedicated, packed like sand in a bag,
we stood straight like the white Englishmen,
we stood like soldiers although we were only boys.

We bore our guns on our shoulders,
we did "Quick march!" even without knowing it,
"Present arms" – we held our guns upright against our foreheads.
"Attention!" – we stood like cows being milked;
we travelled through many lands until we reached Egypt,
Benghazi we entered as a regiment.

We blacks were combatants,
we wrestled with the Italians,
we could hear their aircraft passing by
being chased by sky rockets,
tearing them in mid-flight,
we saw a glimpse of something letting go of its wings.

We heard Hitler praising himself,
declaring that he was the lightning that frightens nations
and causes women to cry.
We said to him, "Defeat you will see with your eyes,
with your hands you will never touch victory":
the buttocks of the Germans began to shiver!

Our spears brought people together,
they brought Mussolini and Japan together,
they destroyed people the way buffaloes do,
they roasted Hitler like a mopani worm;

Ka jeno ntwa ga eyo, go ituletswe fela;
Bairakgang ga bayo, ba iphile lefela.

today the war is over; there is ease;
the proud are no longer there, defeated by their vanity.

Translated from Setswana by David wa Maahlamela
and Tšepiso Samuel Mothibi

Umkhosi wemiDaka

SEK Mqhayi

"Ndim, musan' ukoyika."

Awu! Ewe, kambe siyabulela!
Lakuth' ikokwethu lisicinge,
Ngokuya kusebenz' emazibukweni,
Ngexesha lalo lokuxakeka.

Besingoobani na thina boomthina,
Ukuba singanced' uKumkani weBritani,
Ingangalal' engatshonelwa langa,
Int' elawula umhlaba nolwandle?
Kungoku nesibhakabhak' isingxamele.
Niyeva ke, madodana, niphakamile!
Isizwe senu sisemqulwini wezizwe.
Ze niguye, ze niqambe:
Nenjenje, nenjenje! Nenjenje, nenjenje!
Nenjenje, nenjenje! Nenjenje, nenjenje!

Xa nithul' umthwalo wenqanawa,
Ze nicace, ninganqeni;
Az' omny' avele ngapha, omny' avele ngapha,
Omny' athi khu ngapha, omnye ngapha,
Ewe, *man*, niyisike ithi tyu.
Xa nithul' intsimbi, *man*,
Ze niyibambe ngeengal' ezingenamkhinkqi,
Nime ngemilenze engenankantsi, *man*,
Niyithi hlasi, niyenjenje,

Black soldiers

SEK Mqhayi

"It's me; don't be afraid."

Awu! Yes, we are grateful indeed!
We were thought about in the offices,
to go and work on the estuaries and harbours,
during these difficult times.

Who are we, such as we are,
to help the king of Britain,
a man of high esteem not hindered even by the sunset,
the man who rules the earth and the sea?
He is hurrying to rule over the sky as well.
Do you hear, young men? You have been raised up!
Your nation is listed in the book of nations.
You must sing, you must begin:
I like this – like this! Like this – like this!
Like this – like this! Like this – like this!

When offloading the ship,
you should be visible, and not laze around;
and one of you should be on this side, and another one on that side,
one should move to this side and another to that side,
ja, man, do the right thing.
When you offload steel, *man*,
you should hold onto it even if your arms cramp,
your legs should not tremble, *man*,
grab it like this,

Nithi ho-ha-heje-e-e!
Le'mgo, wha-a-a!

Maze xa nithul' idamaneti,
Nokuba yifiyose nerhuluwa,
Nokuba yigesi nesalfure,
Nokuba yiyiphi n' int' enomlilo,
Niyithi chu ngobunono,
Ukuz' ingabi nangozi;
Ith' ukuba ithe omnye yamluma,
Yamtshisa, yamthini na,
Nisuke nimyaleze kooyise,
Ngenkonz' ephakame kunene;
Nenjenje, nenjenje!
Nenjenje, nenjenjeya!

Maze nimbambe uKeyizare, nize naye,
Iphele le mfazwe ngephanyazo.
Sizokudla noKeyizare iindaba,
Simbalisel' umhla waseSandlwana,
Simbalisel' umhla waseThaba Ntshu,
Simbalisel' umhla waseMthontsi,
Simbalisel' umhla waseGwadana.
Nith' ukuya kumbamba niye ngobulumko.
Niqhel' ukubamb' ingonyam' ihleli;
Nenjenje, nenjenje! Nenjenje, nenjenje!
Nenjenje, nenjenje! Nenjenje, nenjenjeya!

Maze nimgcin' uzepelin phezulu,
Ath' akuphos' umlilo, nimphosele ngezulu;
Ath' akuthob' ityhefu, nithob' umgubo kaPhezulu;
Ath' akwenza ngegesi, nenze ngeenyosi;

and say, "Put it here – put it the-e-e-re!
Let 'im go! – Wha-a-a!"

When you offload dynamite,
whether it's fuses and gunpowder,
whether it's gas or sulphur,
whatever explosive thing it is,
hold it with the utmost care,
so that it does not endanger you.
But if it happens to bite
and kill, do whatever you can,
so that he is welcome with the forefathers,
through the high quality of your ritual:
like this – like this!
Like this – like that!

You should capture the Kaiser and bring him here,
so that this war can end immediately;
so that we can share news with the Kaiser,
and tell him of the day of Isandlwana,
and tell him of the day of Thaba 'Nchu,
and tell him of the day of Thontsi,
and tell him of the day of Gwadana.
Go and seize him with perceptive wisdom.
Of course, you are used to capturing live lions.
And you do it like this – like this! Like this – like this!
Like this – like this! Like this – like that!

Keep an eye on the Zeppelin in the sky,
when it throws fire, you throw lightning;
when it throws poison, you throw herbal powder!
When it uses gas, you use bees;

Ath' akuxakeka, akuxakeka,
Akuxakeka, akuxakeka,
Nimvele ngapha, nimvele ngapha!
Nenjenje ukumqhawula, nimrhangqe,
Nenjenje, nenjenje, nenjenjeya!

Maze nibe neliso kuVon Hindonbere.
Yimfene leyo, ze nize niyikhwele.

Kubizwe nina nje, kubizw' abokugqibela.
Ihlaz' enilenzileyo ze ningezi nalo;
Ubugwal' enibenzileyo ningabuyi nabo.
Ze niyidumis' iAfrika ezizweni;
Nizidumis' iinkosi zenu kanjalo.
Azifananga zanikhupha; ziyazidla ngani.
Ze niwuthobel' umthetho nommiselo.
Wakuw' umthetho ze nenjenje,
Nenjenje, nenjenje, nenjenjeya!

Ze niyidumis' iAfrika ngobukroti.
Ze niyidumis' iAfrika ngamandla.
Ze niyidumis' iAfrika ngokuvisisana,
Niyidumis' iAfrika ngempilo,
Ngobukhali beliso nobendlebe,
Ngokuzinza kwengqondo nobuchopho,
Ngokuthetha, nokuhamba, nokwenza.
Tyhini le! Nisuke nenjenje, nenjenje!
Nenjenje, nenjenjeya!

Hambani ke, bafondini, niye eFransi,
Nikhumbul' indlala eniyishiy' emakhaya.
Izihendo zongendawo zenizoyise,
Kuba nilapho nje, namhla nibingiwe.

when it becomes confused and busy – be busy!
Be confused! Be busy!
Approach it on this side, stick it in from that side!
And head it off – and surround it,
and do it like this – like this – like that!

Keep an eye on the Hindenburgh:
it is a baboon, that one, you should ride on it.

You have been called as a last resort;
if you disgrace yourself there, don't bring disgrace back;
if you were cowards there, don't bring cowardice back.
You should make Africa worthy of praises
and make its chiefs worthy of praises as well.
They did not just hand you over – they are proud of you.
Obey the law and the military orders.
When the law is passed do this,
do this – do this – and do that!

Glorify Africa for its courage,
glorify Africa for its strength,
glorify Africa for its working together,
and glorify Africa for its fitness.
For its sharp eye and ear,
for its stable mind and intellect,
for speaking, walking and taking action,
yes, of course! Just do this – do this!
Do this – and do that!

Go to France, men,
and remember the poverty you left at home.
Overcome the sins of Satan, who is everywhere,
because by being there, you are offering a sacrifice;

Sinenz' idini lesizwe sikaNtu.

Hambani, mathol' eemaz' ezimabele made.

Hambani, mathol' ooNyongande kudlelana.

Hambani, kuba le nto thina sesiyibonile;

UThixo wakowethu seleyijikele ngaphambili.

Hambani ngemilenz' engenamkhinkqi;

Hambani ngeentliziyo ezingenadyudyu;

Ngomzimb' okhaphukhaphu, ngomzimb' ongenantaka,

Nithi gxanya, gxanya, gxanya!

Nithi ngxi-ngxi, ngxi-ngxi!

Nithi ngxi-ngxi, ngxi-ngxilili!

we are making you the sacrifice of the black nation.

Go, calves of sought-after cows with long, easy-to-milk teats;

go, calves of generous mothers;

go, because we have already seen this.

Thixo is walking in front of you.

Go with legs that are not trembling;

go with hearts that are not afraid;

go with a lithe body, with a brave body,

and walk fast, take long strides!

And stand firm, stand firm!

Stand firm, stand very firm!

Translated from isiXhosa by Thokozile Mabeqa

Imbongikazi no*Abantu Batho*

Nontsizi Mgqwetho

Uqhekeko lukaMaxeke! Nokuya kweMbongikazi:

Timbilili! Watsho okade elele
    Wabuya wavuka.
    Timbilili! Watsho okade enetha,
    Intaka yeendada zaseAfrika.

Hawulele! Nto kaMvabaza,
    Namhla isikhumba se*Congress*
    Ngathi sisongwa
    Sisombuluka.

Kudala, Mvabaza, ndakubonayo.
    Uyimazi elubisi luncinanana
    Olungasafikiyo
    Nasezimvabeni.

Hawulele! Hule!
    Wena *Abantu Batho*
    Wawuba uyakusala
    Negama lobugosa.

UMthetheli waBantu
    Kudala akubonayo.
    Uyimvaba engenawo namanzi
    Eyode izale oonojubalalana.

Abantu bayaphela
    Kukufunzwa eweni,

The female poet and *Abantu Batho*

Nontsizi Mgqwetho

Maxeke's breakaway! And the goings on of the female poet:

Wake up! So said the one who was asleep
and then woke up.
Wake up! So said the soldier tested by storms,
the bird from the bushes of Africa.

Greedy one! Son of Mvabaza,
today the cowhide of the Congress,
which held it together,
has been torn apart.

All along, Mvabaza, I have seen what you're up to!
You are a cow with only droplets of milk
that cannot even fill
the goatskin sack.

Greedy one! Whore!
You *Abantu Batho*,
you thought you'd inherit
the title of leader.

A people's spokesperson,
they saw you long ago;
you're a goatskin sack that doesn't even have water in it,
which will eventually breed tadpoles.

People are being annihilated,
being led over a cliff,

Kuba abanamnyangi
Obabhulel' imithi.

Imbongikazi iyile?
Ndandiza kukusukela phi?
Kuba kwelo phepha lakho
Ndoginywa yimilomo yeengonyama.

Ndiyazi, wena Mvabaza,
Akuvumani nelanga,
Kuba waqhel' inyanga,
Into ohamba nayo.
Phawula, mfundi.

Imbongikazi iyile?
Akusazi, Mvabaza, isiXhosa?
Khawufunde kwakhona izibongo
Zoqhekeko lwekhongresi.

Iminyanya yakowethu
Ayibambani neyexelegu.
Ndandithetha ukuthini
Xa ndandisitsho?

Wena Mvabaza, uluyengeyenge
Olweza luphethwe ngesikotile,
Lwafika eRhawutini,
Lwabona soluyinkokeli.

Akuyiyo ke inkokeli
Nakanye, wena Mvabaza,
Ungumrhwebi
Elona gama lakho.

for they do not have a healer
who will prepare medicine for them.

Has the female imbongi gone?
Where should I follow you to?
If I followed your newspaper,
I would be swallowed by lions.

I know you, Mvabaza,
you can't stand the sun
because you are used to the moon,
your companion.
Take note, reader.

Has the female imbongi gone?
Mvabaza, don't you understand isiXhosa?
Read the poems again
about the breakaway from the Congress.

Our ancestors
do not consort with the unclean –
what did I mean
when I said that?

You, Mvabaza, you're a weakling
who was brought on a platter
to Johannesburg
and woke up as a leader.

You are therefore not a leader,
not at all, Mvabaza,
you are a trader;
that is your real name.

Yekana noMfu. Maxeke.
>NguThixo oseke elaa phepha
>Ebona ukuphela kwabantu
>Kukufunzwa eweni.

Ngubani owakubeka
>Ukuba ube yinkokeli?
>Zikhona nje iinkosi
>Ezadalwa nguThixo.

Akuyazi, wena Mvabaza,
>Nendalo kaThixo.
>Naku nam sowundenza
>Imbong'kazi ka-*Abantu Batho*.

Uyavuya wena weza
>Nembongikazi eNgqushwa
>Ukuba mayizokukwenzela
>Isonka eRhawutini
>>Sakubona.

Sifunze kakubi,
>Sifuna izibuko.
>Abantu bayaphela
>Kukufunzwa eweni.

Hawulele! Hule!
>Funz' eweni baseJepe
>Abamemeza ingqina
>Kodwa bengayiphumi.

Leave Reverend Maxeke alone;
it is God who founded that newspaper
on seeing that people were being annihilated
from being led over a cliff.

Who installed you
as a leader?
While the chiefs are still here,
who were created by God.

You definitely don't understand
God's creation, Mvabaza,
even me, you're trying to make me
Abantu Batho's female imbongi.

Shame on you who came
with a female poet from Peddie,
so that she may provide
for you in Johannesburg:
who do you think you are?

We are setting ourselves on your tracks,
we are seeking a place of crossing –
the people are being annihilated
from being led over a cliff.

Greedy one! Whore!
Instigators from Jeppe
who agitate for the hunt,
but do not take part in it.

Zinani ezi nkokeli
  Le nto zingafiyo?
  Zimana zibulalisa
  Abantu bakaThixo namakosi.
    Yimpi kaBheyele.

Yatshona iAfrika
  Ngofunz' eweni,
  Utsho obonga engqungqa
  Engcwabeni likayise.
    Hawuhule!

What's wrong with these leaders?
They do not die,
but they keep causing the deaths
of the chiefs and God's people,
they are Bailey's impi.

Down goes Africa!
Because of the instigators,
so says the female poet who sings praises while she dances
on her father's grave.
Oh, you whore.

Translated from isiXhosa by Zukile Jama and Loyiso Mletshe

Lithothokiso tsa Moshoeshoe le tse ling

DCT Bereng

1

Tsohle li re seleballetse:

Kantle re bona tse makatsang,

Bahlabani ba tlala, ba hlaba fatše.

Letsatsi le chaba botala;

Le hana ho chabela fatše.

Le otlile litlhorong tsa matlo.

Likhomo li hana ho tsoa ka masaka;

Le matšoanafike h'a k'a b'a lla,

Bo bile ba oela fatše.

Nonyana li hana ho fofa,

Li qotoma, li phahama feela.

Na ekaba mehlolo ea kajeno ke ea'ng?

2

Khopolo ea Moshoeshoe e ntšisinya 'mele,

Ke sitoa le ho ahlama ke bua,

Ke ahlama ho bolelisa liketso,

Ke bolela mesebetsi,

Ke bua ka tšoanelo tsa Re-kholo.

Moea oa ka o sisimohela liketso;

Ka lithothokiso ke reneketsa meetlo

Ea Mohale, mohlabani, Moren'a ratehang,

Ea mor'a Mokhachane, mohlank'a sechaba.

3

Sechaba ka matlotlosia se okamela Morena,

Sechaba ka meokho se qaphaletsa Morena;

Se qaphaletsa topo sa mohlabani ea renneng,

The poems of Moshoeshoe and others: extracts

DCT Bereng

1

Everything turned into grief for us:
outside we see only the astonishing;
the warriors prance, they stab the ground.
The sun dawns in reed-green;
it refuses to shine on the ground.
It hits only the peaks of houses.
The cattle refuse to leave their kraals;
even the orange-wing-tipped starlings of dawn don't call,
they flounder, even fall to the ground.
The birds refuse to take flight,
they lift themselves short distances into the air.
To what can all these mysteries of the day be ascribed?

2

The memory of Moshoeshoe shivers through my body,
I am too burdened to speak,
I open my mouth to praise his acts,
I want to mention his great works,
I want to do justice to our Big One.
The Soul-of-Mine shudders at his acts;
with poetry, I praise the habits
of the Warrior, the Spear, the beloved King,
the son of Mokhachane, the servant of the people.

3

The nation in a silent mass attends the wake of the King,
the people splash their tears over the King;
they splash them over the remains of the Great Warrior who reigned,

Se qaphaletsa topo se hlatsuoang sa Khosi.

Topo sa Khosi ha se hlatsuoe ka metsi.

Ka likhapha, phororo tsa meokho,

Re hlatsoa Morena.

Ka pohomel'a lillo tsa sechaba,

Re hlatsoa Hosi.

Ka masoabi re tšoara 'mele oa Morena;

Re o hlatsoa, re o tolisa 'mele oa Morena.

Ka matsoho a thothomelang re ama setopo.

Morena re hlatsoetsa lehl'onolo baneng;

Re tolisetsa melemo sechabeng.

Sechaba, bana ho Morena,

Bana, sechaba ho Morena;

Lehlo'nolo bohlale, kelello ea Morena.

4

Ha re epela Moshoeshoe.

Kharebe li ithiba lifahleho ka masira,

Ha re epela Moshoeshoe.

Nōka li khutsa ho phalla,

Ha re epela Morena.

Meru e emisa ho tsukutleha

Ha re epela Morena.

Tsatsi le tima bohale

Ha re epela Moshoaila.

Lefatše la tlala lerōle

Ha re epela Morena.

Holimo la luma le sele

Ha re epela Morena,

Re epela ea hlōtseng,

Re epela mohale oa senatla,

Eo re khakeletsang khotso ka liatla.

they splash them over the royal remains as they are washed.
The royal remains of the King are not washed with water,
they are washed with a deluge of tears;
we bathe the King.
With laments, with wailings of the nation,
we bathe His Majesty.
With sorrow, we touch the body of the King;
we wash, we bathe the body of the King,
with trembling hands, we touch the remains.
Beloved King, we wash fortune off onto our children;
we wash it off onto the nation.
The nation, children to the King,
the children, nation to the King;
praising him, we receive the virtues of our King.

4

We dig Moshoeshoe's grave.
Virgins cover their faces in veils,
when we dig Moshoeshoe's grave.
Rivers silence their flow,
when we dig the grave of the King.
The forests stop swaying,
when we dig the grave of the King.
The sun snuffs its fierce power,
when we dig the grave of Moshoaila.
The earth fills up with dust,
when we dig the grave of the King.
Thunder rolls in a peculiarly clear sky,
when we dig the grave of the King.
We dig for him who conquered,
we dig for Mohale, our giant,
with both hands, he scooped peace into our palms.

Re epela Thesele'a Matlama.

Phoofolo li lesa ho fula

Ha re epela Morena.

Ka pelo tse sisang

Re epa mobu ho epela Khosi;

Ka meokho ea lillo re pata Morena.

Ka lerata la seboko re pata Morena;

Ka pelo tse bohloko re pata Morena.

Basali ba itšela marama ka likhapha

Ha re pata Morena.

Kharebe li ithiba lifahleho ka masira

Ha re pata Mohale.

Methepa ea lesa ho bonya

Mohla ho lluoang,

Ho lleloa Moren'a naha ea heso,

Morena oa barui le mafutsana.

Nōka li khutsa ho phorohla

Ha re epa ntlo ea Khosi.

Meru, thabeng, ea thola tuu!

Le lehlokoa ho sisinyeha

Mohla re patang Moshoeshoe.

Litlama li emisa ho mela,

Ha re pata Khosi.

Nonyana tsa khaotsa ho bina

Ha re pata Morena.

"Khotso!" ho rialo sechaba phupung ea Morena.

"Pula!" se nahana Morena o tla e nesa.

"Nala!" se re a se kōpele khora Balimong.

5

Na le re ke Thesele'a Mollo?

Na le re Moshoeshoe o shoele?

We dig for Thesele of Matlama, the Great Binder-Together.
Animals cease their grazing,
when we dig the grave of the King.
With hearts that are sighing,
we dig the soil to make the King's grave;
with tears of lament, we bury the King.
With the wild wailing of those who love him, we bury the King;
with painful hearts, we bury the King.
Women drench their cheeks in tears,
when we bury the King.
Girls hide their faces in veils,
when we bury Mohale.
Young maidens stop smiling
when there is so much wailing,
mourning for the King of my land,
a king for the rich and the poor.
Rivers quieten their torrents,
when we dig the grave of His Majesty.
Forests, they hush on the mountain!
Not even the grass sways
the day we bury Moshoeshoe.
The herbs stop sprouting,
when we bury the King.
The birds stop singing,
when we bury the King.
"Peace!", says the nation at the funeral of the King.
"Rain!" – thinking the King will make it fall.
"Prosperity!" – exhorting him to beg for abundance from the
    Ancestors' heaven.

5

Do you say this is Thesele of Fire?
Do you really say Moshoeshoe is dead?

Le re ke een'a siileng chaba sa hae?
Le re Moren'a ka siea chaba sa hae,
  A se siea a falla?
Chaba seo a se loanetseng nto'a mali,
Ha thebe li ne li khantšetsana 'mala,
Marumo a bina ije-ijelele hlohong tsa lira;
A bina pina tsa ntoa ho banna maphakong?
  Ao, che, ke ea hana!
Ha le bolele mor'a Mokhachane!
A ke ke a shoa chaba sa phela.
Se phelela'ng eena a shoele?
A ke ke a shoa chaba sa phela.
Le epetse masapo, Morena oa phela.
Ho phela ntlo ea Moshoeshoe.
Khosi ha e'a shoa, e robetse;
Empa Morena h'a robale e se ngoana,
O ea falla.

6

O ile ea matla mohale,
Moroba rumo la Chaka a b'a le khomeletse.
Thabeng, ka molao li ka be li ngotsoe.
Tsa hae liketso, li hlōtse.
Ha li na ea ho li pheta kheleke;
Ea ho bolela meetlo ka mathathamo,
Ea ho pheta tšebetso tsa hlale ba hae,
Ha e eo eo kheleke.
Ha se s'o be teng seqapi
Sa ho bina mehlolo ka qoqotho,
Se etsa bokheleke ka molomo.
Nonyana lia bina, lia tsoelikanya;
Empa Moshoeshoe na lia 'mina?

Do you say it is he who has left his people?
Do you say the King has abandoned his subjects,
left them for good?
The people he fought for with blood,
when shields flashed their colours to each other,
when spears sang "ije-ijelele", chants of death against the heads of
   the enemy,
singing songs of war to men on the flanks?
Awu, really, I refuse!
You do not mean the son of Mokhachane!
He cannot die but the people live.
Why should they live if he is dead?
He won't die while the nation survives.
You have buried only the bones: the King lives.
On lives the house of Moshoeshoe.
His Majesty is not dead, he is sleeping;
but the King does not sleep, for he is not a child;
he simply migrates.

6

He is gone now, the strong warrior,
the breaker of Shaka's assegai, binding it to others.
In the mountain, this should be written as law.
His deeds, they are victorious.
No praise singer is eloquent enough to describe them;
to plumb the hierarchies of his habits,
to recount the extent of his wisdom,
there is no such praise singer.
There is no larynx capable
of singing from the throat these miracles,
performing the eloquence of them with the mouth.
The birds sing, their notes intertwine and break into each other;
but nothing and nobody can sing Moshoeshoe's song to the end.

7

Ke efe Khosi e hlōtseng Thesele,
E mo haisitseng ka matla boreneng,
E mo hlōlisitseng ka ho ratoa,
E mo tsielitseng ka bohlale,
Le ka lerato ho sechaba,
Le ka botumo lichabeng?
Hoba, utloang, chaba ha se so mo lebale!

8

Mona ho phomotse Thesel'a Matlama.
A ke a be boiketlong ba tlōtleho,
Morena, mobung oa naha ea hae!
Morena oa toka e seng tšobotsi;
'Nete, e seng leeme.
Ba ikokotletseng ka eena ba lehlohonolo;
Ba fumane boitšetleho lereng la khotso.
Ka eena litsohatsana li kokorohile,
Tsa itebala mengoaha bongata,
Tsa itebala meriri boputsoa,
Tsa re 'mala ke letšoao.

O robetse 'Mokelli oa basōtlehi,
Eena 'Musi oa Basotho le Matebele,
Mofani oa limpho tsa Borena.
Bohle ka tsoho le fanang a ba abela.
Pelo ea hae, lere la ba fokolang.

7

What King ever defeated Thesele-the-Battering-Ram,
who surpassed His Majesty in kingship,
who surpassed him in being loved,
who surpassed him in wisdom,
even in love for his subjects,
even in fame among other nations?
Because – listen – his people will never forget him!

8

Here rests the Battering-Ram-of-Matlama.
Let him be in the comfort of the glory due to him,
a king, in the soil of his land,
a king of goodness that was never a pretence
of truth, that had no partiality.
Those who lean on him are fortunate;
they have found repose in the sceptre of peace.
Through him, the aged have found a walking stick –
they forget their many years,
they forget the blue in their hair,
the colour marking old age.

He has gone to sleep now, the Conqueror-of-Our-Plight,
He, the Ruler of Basotho and Matebele,
the giver of the gifts of kingship.
He distributed fairly with a hand that was used to giving.
His heart, the staff of the weak.

Mona ho robetse ea kentseng leseli lefifing,
Matla le lere la Basotho,
Mothei le moahi oa Lesotho.
Khotso! Pula! Nala! Naheng ea Basotho.

Here now sleeps one who brought light to the darkness,
the strength and the staff of the Basotho rests,
the founder and builder of Lesotho.
Peace! Rain! Prosperity! In the land of the Basotho.

Translated from Sesotho by Tšepiso Samuel Mothibi

Kgosi Tshaka

LD Raditladi

Kobekgolo ya Mozulu mathatha,
Batho ba yone ba ntse ba sa botha,
Batho ba yone ba tletse lefatshe,
Ba bolaile e seng ka dimpa di kgotshe.
Mozulu yo o tlhomile a dira sekai,
E le tselanyana e sa welweng ditlai,
Segai sa gagwe sa gabaka batho,
Tshaka ya rema dikgata tsa batho,
Ya phunya mogodu wa lesea tharing,
Ya runa letsetse le nta moriring.

Matsibogwana a nna bophalaphala,
Madi a tlalatlala a tlhabisa kgala,
Taukgolo ya kona batho dihuba,
Ba tlhoka go mmolelela ditšhaba;
Ntšwa tsa gabalatsega ditlharapa,
Tsa baa tsa namalatsa nko di dupa.
Tshaka, o ka bo o rebotse le Mathosa,
Ga ba kitla ba kgona go go losa,
O ka bo o ba reboletse go tshela,
Batlhanka ba kgwadibane ba phela.

Kgabo e kile ya atolola lenaga,
Ya phunyega jaaka phefo mariga,
Merole ya tetesela melapong,
Kgabo ya tsena mathaka marapong,
Ba gakwa fela, ba etsa maatlhamana,
Go thibela mmofolela go tsena.
Banna ba sitwa ba ama direpodi,

King Shaka

LD Raditladi

That imposing Zulu leopard skin is trouble,
its people are never at rest,
they are spread over the land,
they have not massacred with empty stomachs.
That Zulu was setting an unforgettable example,
he was a path that could not be travelled,
his assegai pulverised people's skulls,
Shaka harvested people's skins,
he drilled into the unborn baby's stomach in the womb,
crushing the lice and fleas in its hair.

Drifts of rivers were overflowing,
blood spilling in torrents,
the big lion squashed people's chests,
they no longer feared his vision;
the dogs had ribs stretching out like dry branches,
but they were still alive, still sniffing.
Shaka, you should have left the Xhosas alone,
they could not afford to attack you,
you should have allowed them to live,
so that the servants of the sea turtle could survive.

A flame then swept the veld,
piercing like the cold winds of winter,
calves shivered next to the river beds,
the flame penetrated people's bones,
the living just gave up,
they could no longer protect themselves from freezing.
Men were too cold to tend to their work,

Ba sitwa le ke go gama dipodi,
Ba re di fusitse ba sa di thetsa,
Ka letshogo dilo le di retetsa.

Batho baagwe ba swafolaswafola,
Ba dira jaaka matlhalerwa fela,
Ba phura batho ba etsa dibatana,
Tshaka ya agwe ya kgethanya marena,
Kgosikgolo, o ka bo o sa ba kgekgetha,
Wa gataka maoto a batho ba kgetha,
Wa gapa tse di makoro di lema.
O koo o editse Mosotho le Kgama
O ka bo jaanong o agetswe moduku
Ke lefikantswe le le kgabuduku.

they were unable to milk goats,
the goats ceased to give milk when their udders were not kneaded,
fear prevented the men from completing their tasks.

Some people were ripping others apart,
devouring them like hyenas,
crushing people's bones like beasts.
Shaka's spear divided the kingdoms;
oh, Great One, you shouldn't have slaughtered them,
flattening people who were paying taxes,
plundering their ploughing cattle.
You should have been like Moshoeshoe and Kgama;
then you would now have a monument,
a memorable, precious gravestone.

Translated from Setswana by Stephen Masote,
David wa Maahlamela and Tšepiso Samuel Mothibi

Aa! Zweliyazuza, itshawe laseBhilitani!

SEK Mqhayi

NguMzimb' uyaqhuma elokubuliswa;
NguMzimb' uyavutha elomteketiso;
NguZweliyazuz' elibizwa ngasemva;
NguTshawuz' imiban' elibizwa yimbongi.
    Sinika!

Phumani nonke, nize kufanekisa!
Phumani, zizwe nonke, nize kufanekisa!
Sisilo sini n' esi singaziwayo,
Singajongekiyo, singaqhelekiyo?
Yaz' ithi kanti yile nabulele,
Isilokaz' esikhulu seziziba.
Yaz' ithi kanti ngulo Makhanda-mahlanu,
Inyok' enkul' eza ngezivuthevuthe.
Yaz' ithi kanti ngulo Gilikankqo,
Isil' esikhul' esingaziwa mngxuma.
Le nt' umzimb' uyaqhuma ngathi liziko;
Le nt' umzimb' uyavutha ngathi lidangatye;
Le nt' iqhuqhumb' iintlantsi ngathi nguSindiya-ndiya;
Le nt' itshawuz' imibane ngathi sisibhakabhaka.
    Sinika!

Nalo lisiz' iTshawe leBhilitani:
Inzala yenyathikaz' uVitoliya,
Inkazan' ebuThixorha kwizwe lakwaNtu,
Ebumoyarha, butolorha, bugqirharha.
Nants' isiz' inkwenkwe kaJoji wesihlanu;
Yez' emadodeni inkwenkw' akomkhulu:
Umdak' oliso litshawuz' imibane,

Aa! Hail, Unsettling Country, you hero of Britain!

SEK Mqhayi

Hail! Smouldering Body, hero of Britain!
In greeting him, we call him Body-as-Hot-as-Flame.
In private, we dub him Unsettling Country;
Praising him, the imbongi calls him Lightning-That-Flashes.
     We greet you!

Hey, come out everyone and judge for yourself!
Come out, all nations, and see for yourself!
Hey, what kind of creature is this
that our eyes can't behold him, that we can't get used to him?
Perhaps he is that ancient monster Nabulele,
that enormous animal of the deep pools,
living with five heads like Makhanda-mahlanu.
Oh, the snake arrives with explosive force.
Maybe it's even Gilikankqo,
too big to be known by any lair.
Smoke rises from his body like a fireplace.
Flames shoot from his body like a fire.
Sparks spit from the body like a come-and-go steam engine.
Lightning flashes from the body as if it is the universe.
     We greet you!

Here he comes, the hero of Britain,
the son of the she-buffalo, Victoria,
a woman like a god in the country of men,
a mystical, supernatural warrior-priestess.
Here he comes, the young son of George the Fifth,
this son of the royal household coming to the circle of men,
dun-coloured man whose eyes shoot out lightning.

Lithi lakujezul' ung' ungaphanyaza,
Umdak' osabuphotyo-butyatho,
Unga nganabomi wakuwondela.
Kok' ithol' lerhamncw' alondeleki,
Nabakhe balinga bajub' isiduli.
Yez' inkwenkw' omgquba yomthonyama!
Yez' ixhom' izindwe, yaxhom' ugijo;
Yez' ifak' umnzunga, yafak' iphunga;
Yez' itsho ngezidanga nezidabane;
Yez' itsho ngobumbejewu bobuhlalu;
Yez' inobulawu nobuqholo;
Yez' inetyeleba nezifikane;
Yez' inomtho nomthombothi;
Yeza ngobungwe nobungwenyama;
Yeza bugcolocho buchoko-chokozo!
Sinika, Lawundini!

Tarhu, Bhilitan' eNkulu,
Bhilitan' eNkul' engatshonelwa langa!
Siya kumthini na lo mntwan' oKumkani?
Siya kumthini na lo mntwan' oMhlekazi?
Khaniphendule, nani zintaba zezwe lethu!
Nani milambo yakowethu, khanithethe!
Maz' aselwandle, khanimthule kambe.
Mthuleni, maz' azelwandle,
Sikhe simbone, simjonge, simlozele.
Ibilapha nenkwenkwez' enomsila.
Angaba yen' usekhondweni layo.
Ibize kwabakwaPhalo kaTshiwo;
Ibize kumaZulu, kubeSuthu;
Ibize kumaSwazi, kubaTshwana;
Ibilundwendwe losapho lukaNtu!

When his dazzling gaze strikes you, it strikes you blind.

When you look at him, his eyes are vivid creatures looking back
at you.

No one can behold this calf of a wild animal.

Those who dare to look at him are struck unconscious.

Here comes the child of the deepest manure in the royal cattle
kraal!

He comes, bearing the rank of a crane feather, his chest adorned
with beautiful, rare beadwork.

He comes in the red ornaments of an exuberant initiate;

He comes in a splendid vestment and a cloak of dressed oribi skin.

He comes with alluring incense.

He comes oozing the perfume of a chief.

He comes exuding the fragrance of thyme and aromatic herbs.

He comes radiating the scent of mint and tamboti.

He comes treading proudly like a lion.

He comes, stepping stealthily like a leopard on his claws.

    Greet him, you philistine!

Hail, Great Britain!

The Britain over which the sun never sets.

What are we going to do with this kingly child?

What are we going to do with the son of His Handsomeness?

Lift up your voices, mountains of my country!

And you, rivers, speak to me!

Waves of the sea, drop him here

so that we can inspect him thoroughly!

Study him, study him from head to toe.

The comet passed us once.

Can it be that he is also tracing that star with the tail?

That comet visited us here, the people of Phalo, son of Tshiwo.

It visited the Zulu and the Sotho.

Kub' uYehov' uThix' uyalawula,
Uyathetha ngendalo yakhe.
Uyawakhawulezis' amaxesh' akhe!

Tarhu, Langaliyakhanya!
Uphuthum' inkwenkwezi yakowenu na?
Thina singumz' owab' iinkwenkwez' akowenu.
Simbambana ngeSilimela thina,
Yona nkwenkwezi yokubal' iminyaka,
Iminyaka yobudoda, yobudoda!

Hay' kodw' iBritan' eNkulu –
Yeza nebhotile neBhayibhile;
Yeza nomfundis' exhag' ijoni;
Yeza nerhuluwa nesinandile;
Yeza nenkanunu nemfakadolo.

Tarhu, Bawo, sive yiphi na?
Gqithela phambili, Thol' esilo,
Nyashaz' ekad' inyashaza!
Gqitha, uz' ubuye kakuhle,
Ndlalifa yelakowethu.
Makadl' ubom uKumkani!
Ndee ntsho-ntshobololo!
Ngokwalaa nkwenkwezi yayinomsila!

It visited the Swazi and the Tswana.
The star made a pilgrimage to the humanity of Africa!
Because the living God reigns and He speaks truth through his
   creation.
He lets time run quickly.

Hail, Sun-That-Is-Shining!
Have you come to look for your star?
Don't you know that we are the people who distribute the stars?
There on that side is the morning star, the star of your people.
We bind ourselves and hold on to the Pleiades,
the plough star, the star of June,
the star that counts the years of our manhood.

No, Great Britain!
Here you come with a bottle and a Bible.
Here you come with a preacher arm-in-arm with a soldier.
Here you come with gunpowder and a breech-loader.
Here you come with a cannon and a shotgun.

Help us, oh God, to which one should we yield?
Pass us by, Calf-of-the-Animal,
Trampler who has been trampling forever!
Pass us by and come back nicely,
you who eat the death of our country.
May he eat life, the king!
I've said it; I vanish,
just like that star with a tail.

Translated from isiXhosa by Koos Oosthuysen and Gabeba Baderoon

Sempe a Lešoboro

Michael Ontefetse Martinus Seboni
and Ernest Pelaelo Lekhela

Legougou la lona *dimense*,
E rile go twe *gougou* ka tshoga,
Pelo ya tshoga ya ntika morago
Ke itlhomna lo raya nna ka nosi,
Ntekwane lo re raya, le lona lo itheye
Lo bo lo reye le banyana ba *dimense*.
Ramapotwana o potapota *gaisi*,
O tlhola a tikela mo *gaising*,
Lekobakoba la goora Lešoboro,
Sempe, e kete go bolawa noga,
E bile e kete go bolawa molelemedi,
Le mefinyana ya dilepe e a wa.
Go buile MmaSelemela a re,
"Nnaha Sempe wa ga ka, o bolawa eng?"
A re, "Mma, ke bolawa ke ditšhentšha banna;
Nna ke bolawa ke kgomo ya *pereko*.
Mogolokwane wa lela, wa lela phetelela,
Kwa lwapeng lwa ga MmaSelemela;
A bona Sempe a tla a e kgweetsa,
A re, "Ngwanaka mmentla o humile thata?"
A itumelela go tla a thibile moroba.
Ngwale boela yoo o mmokile,
O boka o sa itse ina la gagwe,
Ina la gagwe ke matsodimatsoke.

Sempe of the Lešoboro clan

Michael Ontefetse Martinus Seboni
and Ernest Pelaelo Lekhela

The Hurry-Up People said,
"Hurry up," to me and I got a fright,
my heart jumped to stand right behind me
because I thought you people were talking only to me like that,
only to find you were also talking to your own like that
and even to your own meisies.
Ramapotwana, the boss, goes round and round his house –
he often disappears into it.
But running around always to do his work
is Sempe of the Lešoboro: as if he is killing a snake,
as if he is busy with a slitherer;
the handle of the axe breaks loose, so hard does he pretend.
MaSelemela speaks and asks,
"What's happening, Sempe, what's bothering you?"
He answers, "Mme, I am being killed by this man-changing thing;
I am being killed by this ox called work."
Ululation breaks loose and lasts a long time,
At the place of MaSelemela.
When people see Sempe driving a heifer,
she asks, "My child, did you work so hard today?"
because he is clearly delighted with the calf.
Young one, relax, you've achieved that,
you've glorified your name without knowing it,
your name is now interwoven like a rope.

Translated from the Setswana
by Stephen Masote and Tšepiso Samuel Mothibi

Sefela

Teboho Raboko

Lumela moo lefu lesesane khomo ea Raboko.
Lefu le ts'etse ka likepe metsing,
Le thoba Rashea.
Le thoba Rashea likepeng koana,
Le thoba botlolong ba le koaletse,
Le kene Maseru Mejametalana.
Paka mots'eare-oa-mantsiboea
Ha basali ba ts'ola liqhaqhabola
Ba ts'ola metoho ea mantsiboea
Maqhotsa a na a re ke bolala sonke.
Basotho ba re ke mokakallane,
Thope li ne li sale li ngannge matsoele,
Banna ba ne ba shoe ba ngannge lifuba.
U ka bona e ne e le sehloho.
...

E tsoa Phaale khomo ena eso,
E tsoa Phaale ha Motaemane koana,
E hlaha koana Nonkokolosa,
E tsoa Marotobolosa,
E tsoa Nonthoboro,
E itsoela koana Namalibuletse.
Metseng e meholo feela,
Moo banna ba teng e leng Baloetsi,
Le basali ba teng e leng Baloetsi,
Bana ba teng ba hlaha e le Baloetsi,
Ke batho ba buang ka lihoana.
Ea re ke fihla le eona pitsi ena ea ka
Bare ts'oene e fepe ena ea ka.

Hymn: extracts

Teboho Raboko

Hail, Thin Death, Bull-of-Raboko.
Death crossed the waters on ships,
it eloped from Russia.
It eloped with those flaking Russian ships,
it eloped with the bottle they closed it in,
it entered Maseru, Place-of-Red-Sandstone.
It arrived in the middle of the afternoon
when women were taking their three-legged pots from the fire
the cooking pots with fermented porridge for the evening.
The Xhosa named it Killing-Everybody.
The Basotho say it is Lying-on-Your-Back-Illness,
young unmarried women die with their breasts bared,
men die with their chests bared.
You can imagine how cruel this is.
…

It comes from Phaale, this cow of home,
it comes from Phaale Ha-Motaemane.
It comes from Nonkokolosa,
it comes from Marotobolosa,
it comes from Nonthoboro,
it comes from Namalibuletse.
it comes from big cities only,
where all the men are patients,
and all the women are patients,
even the babies are patients,
their voices sound as if they are speaking with divining calabashes.
When I arrived with this horse of mine,
they told a perished monkey to feed it.

Eare ts'oene ha e re e isa liatla

Khomo ea ts'oha ea ngoana Raboko.

Ea ts'oaroa ke letope ea thothomela,

Ea baleha ka liqhana le litleleki,

Ke ile ka utloa ka mochana Malika,

A sa fihla a re: Malome Teboho,

Tseba khomo e tseka ke ena,

E eme ka liqhana thoteng,

E ntse e tlola e raha,

E raha, e tseka

E re e palangoe ke Mafereka,

Ke ntat'ae.

Ona ke molie-lie,

Ke lerato la makaako,

Ke la bafo la baikhants'i.

Ke la baikhohomosi morena.

Mohla e n'a be e ts'ela mose maoatleng koana,

E n'a be e palame mohla serame se tsohang se patetse,

Likanono li ne li hana ho sotha melomo,

Meshinikane e ne e hana ho pompa leoatleng le bitsoang
  Rasiti.

Hoa tla hlapi e nyane ea lelinyane,

Tsena tse kholo tsa be se li hlaha,

Lihlapi bo-Shaderaka tsa hlaha li ahlamollaka melomo,

Li lebeletse ha sekepe se teba.

Mali a khomo ena eso a tle a seke a senyeha,

Li tle li eje li e qetele maleng Khanyapa.

Mpepe khomo ea mong a me,

U nkise moo ha ntate ha morena Lesaoana,

Ke utloa ho thoe o fana likhomo

O fana le batho

O fana le bana ba masea.

When the monkey reached out its skeletal palm,
my horse shivered and shied away from the child of Raboko.
It was overcome with tremors and shaking,
it fled with saddle and stirrup,
I heard from the nephew of Malika,
who upon its arrival said, "Uncle Teboho,
the animal with the white blaze is here,
it stands with its saddle in the veld,
and rears, striking with its hoofs,
and kicks, tugging,
indicating that it wants to be mounted by Mafereka,
his father."
This is a game,
it is the love of the vain,
it is of the plebs and the proud.
It is of the conceited, my King.
On the day the ship was crossing over there in the seas,
it was boarded on the day the frost fell hard,
when the tanks could not turn their mouths,
when machine guns did not want to fire in the sea called Rasiti.
Then came this small fry of a ship,
and a big one appeared,
then sharks burst up with open jaws,
waiting as the ship sank.
Blood this red should not be spilt,
now the fish can finish it off in the belly of the leviathan Khanyapa.
Carry me, ox of my master,
take me to my father at Chief Lesaoana's,
I hear it said he offers cattle,
he offers people,
he even offers babies.

Molielie ke oo ke lerato la makaako
Ke la bafo la baikhants'i,
Ke la baikhohomosi.

...

'Mamphielo a ba sa lla,
A re: "Le koana u eang,
Le koana u eang khomo ea Raboroko,
Le koana u eang, u ea ntoeng,
U ea khabong ea marumo a tuka,
Bahale ba koana ntoeng."
Batho ba chele liatla ke bohale ba ntoa.
Matha Fokotsane,
Nyamatsane o fokotse bohale ba thota.
U cheke likoti,
Khomo ea Raboko u cheke likoti.
Thoteng mono metso ea joang u e shebise holimo,
Tsoala tsa joang u li shebise fats'e.
E thume ke eo e ntle e molala o molelele.
Lumela he uena Thuhlo-khoarahla,
Lumela thamaha khaka sepata-mala.
Nonyana ea se-noa-metsi,
E be re metsi a e tabola hloho,
A e otle linkong mona mahananeng,
Banna ba heso ba Ramats'eliso,
Ba re ka Phalima serame se letse metsing,
Ba maoto ba choachoasela monoana.
Ra sea-le-bananyana 'mapalong,
Papaling ea banana le bashanyana.

The game is there, it is the love of the carefree
it is of the plebs and the proud,
it is of the conceited.

…

Mamphielo wailed,
Saying, "Even there where you go,
there where you go, Bull-of-Raboroko,
you fight wars.
You fight in the middle of a blaze of burning spears,
the fierce are in the middle of that war."
The fierceness of this war has burnt people's hands.
Run, Swallow,
dig your hooves into the soil and quell the violence.
Dig holes,
Bull-of-Raboko, dig holes.
Replant the grass with its roots facing up to the sky,
turn the seedpods upside down.
Grind that lovely flower with the long throat.
Greetings to you, Fire-Spotted Giraffe,
Greetings, guinea fowl, Dotted-One-of-Elusive-Colour.
Bird that drinks the waters,
then the water cracks into a comb on its head,
water that beats deep in the sinuses,
men of my home of Ramats'eliso,
we say: in Phalima, the frost is laid on the waters,
the traveller's bare feet itch, his toes burn for the road.
Father of Me-Who-Always-Plays-with-Girls,
yes, the game of girls and boys.

Translated from Sesotho by Tšepiso Samuel Mothibi and Antjie Krog

Mogokgo yo sa rateng tiro

BD Magoleng

Ngwaga o tloga, o lwela "rolo"!
Tloa le tlatswa dikakarapa,
Ditlhapi di balwa ka menwana:
Kolo se tswa kgetsi ya ga Dimo.

Mokganni o tshwere boatla –
Thamaga di gana go goga.
Bontsi di roba dikei –
Maungo go kgotswe makgela!

Moleta g'a arabiwe –
Wa bua, o lwela bogosi.
Motho o akotse segolo,
Puso e okeditse mogolo.

O rwala masigo ka tlhogo,
Go tshosa bafeti ba tsela.
Letona ga a ye tlelaseng –
Ga a itse se se dirwang.

Barutabana ba fatšhwa tsebe –
Ba tshela ka go tetesetswa!
Go sekwa le ditlontlokwane,
Tiro e lebetswe gotlhelele!

Mogokgo yo sa ruteng
Sefofu se se bonang!
O ikgatlha a bolelelwa;
Nama, o kgotso, go direlwa.

The principal who hates his work

BD Magoleng

From the start, he only cares about the roll call!
His net is full of crabs,
the fish can be counted on one hand:
the school is a cannibal's sack of chaos.

This cattle driver is blundering –
his cattle refuse to pull.
They keep on breaking the yokes –
his harvest is fruitless!

This man is a bully –
you talk – you want his position.
His waist is so big –
government increased his salary.

He wears the night on his face,
scaring passers-by.
The headman never visits his class
so he does not know what is happening in his village.

The teachers' ears reverberate with his voice –
they flutter with fear!
Even petty things are disputed,
so the real work never gets done!

The principal who does not teach
is a blind man who can see!
What he desires is being reported to;
meat! And he's at peace. He's been served.

Fa di ile go kgwa mowa,
Moleta o ya go ijela.
O tlhola a imona melomo,
Koko e jewa ka dikuku.

Komiti e tla, o a ngala!
Bokete o bega jwa tiro.
O bega a ntse a eme,
Ga twe dibuka ga di phepa.

Batlhatlhobi ba tla, o dule!
O ile go batla "thitšhere"
Ntekwane go se phatlhatiro –
Mathaithai a ga mogokgo.

During lunch break you can see,
the principal plunges into his plate.
Smack-smacking his lips,
eating chicken and cake together.

When a committee comes, he sulks!
Work! Lots of work! Is his constant complaint.
He reports from the doorway,
stating that finances are not good.

The inspectors are coming? He's out of here!
Saying he is "scouting" for a teacher
even if there is no vacancy –
the shady shenanigans of a lazy principal!

Translated from Setswana by Stephen Masote,
David wa Maahlamela and Tšepiso Samuel Mothibi

Modjadji
Mmapule Emma Ramaila

Modjadji mmala' kgobela,
La kgobela ke lala tsela.
Ke mohlolo 'se na moloti,
Ke lotwa ke mabu a tsela.
Ke Phetole sefetola maru a Tatša,
Ke sefetola morogo ka monwana.
Ke segodi mmabantima maritša,
Dipelo di swere mabolao.
Ke segodi sa mmautlane maeba,
Se utla le dikgakana.

Modjadji ke mphak'a tlou makgolo,
Wa tšwa kgatleng o ja nama.
Wa se je pitsi o ja thutlwa,
Thutlwa mokakatledi mokhufi mmona tša kgole,
Tša kgaufsi a tsatsampela.

Modjadji ke Makaepea ka noši,
Ke Selokelela bana difoto, basadi ba le gona,
Ba tletše motse-mogolo wa Lekhebeleni.
Ke motse wa boMoneri le boMorwatshehla.

Agee... Agaa...! A re yeng kua Bolobedu,
Boloba thakga go lobileng kgomo le motho.
Ga mmamotho ga a hlaolwe, motho go hlaolwa moloi.
Gona kua ga Madumane mefakeng,
Mamatshira thaba ya letšatši ka thoko.

Modjadji

Mmapule Emma Ramaila

Modjadji, the one who counts while gathering,
then you collect, while I hit the road.
I am the miracle without a protector,
I'm protected by the soil of the road.
I am a changer changing clouds at Mount Tatša,
I stir morogo with my finger.
I am the distant eagle, deprived of delicacies,
the hearts hold on to their sleeping places.
I am the eagle, the Killer-of-Doves,
I kill young guinea fowls too.

Modjadji is the knife of the elephant grandmother,
if it comes out of her pocket, it eats meat.
If it doesn't eat the zebra, it eats the giraffe,
the giraffe, the Stretched One, Seer-of-Horizons,
to see what is near, it has to bend.

I, Modjadji, appoint myself,
I am the one who gives bangles to children while women watch,
they fill the large village of Lekhebeleni.
They fill the village of Moneri, the missionaries, and Morwatshehla,
    the sallow ones.

Agee... Agaa...! Let us head for Bolobedu,
place where respect is given to cattle and humans.
Place-of-No-Distinction-Among-Humans, where only witches
    discriminate.
The place of Madumane at the Modjadji palms,
Mamatshira, the mountain with sun on one side.

Ke Maolwe malootšong a diepe

Gabo Malekutu la Matšhweni thibolla mašikišiki,

Meleteng ya diphepheng.

Mokhururung Sehlomamotheka.

Gabo Tumedi le boRamokgwakgwa.

Ke Sehlákong boila kolobe.

Gabo Magobosana a bo Ntshese.

Mošol'a nok' a Masekgatša sa Bakwena.

I am Maolwe, the whetstone for the axes,
place of Malekutu from Open-Up-for-the-Big-Black-Spiders,
at the Holes-of-the-Red-Scorpions.
At Mokhurung, the place where the king is crowned with a feather
  in the hair.
Place of Tumedi-and-them and Ramokgunukgwa-and-them.
This is at Sehlákong, the place of the people of the warthog.
Place of Magobosana-and-them and Ntshese-and-them.
The other side of the river of Masekgatša of the Bakwena.

Translated from Sepedi by Biki Lepota

Morena Maledu (Cecil Rhodes)

NH Kitchin

Ke Maledu, lo ka mmona a betlilwe mo lefikeng,
  A eme gare ga motse mogolo wa Teemaneng,
A tsepegile matlho kgakala a lebile kwa Mafikeng;
  A thothomeditse mogopolo kwa Matebeleng.

O eteletse sešaba sa ga gabo pele jaaka Moshe,
  O tsenye mono a feta a phunya mekoti ya Niberose,
A tsena Bolawane a ba a nama jaaka thotse,
  Bolawane o kakanngwang o tsenwa tšhweetšhwee.

O ntshitse morwa Loapi ka tlhako ya sejaro,
  Lefatshe ja gagwe ba le dira matsankotsanko,
Gompieno gauta le kgotlho di etswa segolo
  Goora Matshobane go etelwa fela ga go poitshego.

O phuntse tsela Maledu, ga go tlhole go belaelwa,
  Le motho a etela goo Moselekatse ga' re oa palelwa.
Dikgetse tsa dipabi di ikhutseditse go sotlhelwa
  Bolawane jaanong ga a tseelwe ngwaga go etelwa.

Ruri pelotshweu e kaiwa e ntsha lobelo!
  Morena Maledu o sule sentle a se na tlhobaelo,
Ka a raladitse lefatshe ja Matebele koloi ya molelo
  Egepeto re tlaa tsamaya re mmona ga go pelaelo.

Chief Cecil Rhodes, the double-chinned one

NH Kitchin

This double-chinned man you see carved here in stone,
   erected here in this diamond town,
he casts his eyes far away to Mahikeng,
   he sends his thoughts north to Matabeleland.

This man led his nation like Moses,
   he drove past here, drilled his way to Niberose,
he entered Bulawayo, he stretched out like a squash vine,
   he settled Bulawayo without turmoil and fuss.

He shifted the soil with his shoes,
   he ripped the land to bits and pieces,
this land that today yields iron and gold,
   so our people can stay here in peace.

He paved the way, this double-chin, silenced complaints;
   Mzilikazi's land is no longer a mess.
We no longer grind our tears for maize
   Bulawayo no longer waits for guests.

Indeed it displays a welcoming heart!
   Chief Cecil died well, untroubled by ghosts,
in his chariot, he took Matebeleland to the world,
   to Egypt: we will meet him there.

Translated from Setswana by David wa Maahlamela and Rita Barnard

UNkosi Rholihlahla Nelson Mandela
(Aa! Zweliyashukuma!)

DLP Yali-Manisi

Ilizwe liyashukuma, maLawundini!
Iintlambo zonke ziyaxokozela;
Iintaba zonke ziyadidizela;
Izizw' ezikhulu zimangalisiwe,
Kuba izizwana ziyagqushalaza.
Ziyaqhashambula, ziyabhinyalaza.
Inen' ilizwe liyashukuma;
Inen' ilizwe liyashukuma!

Aa! Zweliyashukuma!
UZweliyashukuma ngumdaka kaMandela,
Umdak' onobomi wakwaSokhawulela,
KwaDlom' omdlanga, kwaNgqolomsila,
Ingxangxos' ehamba ngamadolo yakwaHala,
Intsimb' edl' ezinye yakwaNdaba.
UKhalamqadi wafa yintsika,
Umty' ondindilili wasemaNtandeni.

Umgawuli wezint' ezisemeveni,
Egec' iintsunguzi zobudenge;
UMavelel' iimbombo zomhlaba;
Uzama-zam' ilizwe lizama-zame;
UMabhijel' ilizwe njengechanti.
Izilenz' elidada kwaweLigwa,
Liye ngokusela kwaweZambesi,
Umkhonzi wezizwe zeAfrika.

Chief Rholihlahla (Bring-Forth-the-Branch)
Nelson Mandela (Hail, Earthquake!)
DLP Yali-Manisi

The earth is shaking, light-skinned ones!
The valleys tremble;
all the mountains shudder;
great nations are astounded;
because the small nations are in tumult –
they are in uproar, struggling to be free.
Truly, the earth quakes;
yes, truly the earth shakes.

Hail, Earthquake!
Earthquake he is, he, the lion-coloured son of Mandela,
lovely tawny-skinned one from the house of Sokhawulela,
at the armed place of Dlomo the dignitary, the place of
  Ngqolomsila,
the secretary bird of Hala that is so tall that he walks on his knees,
the iron that eats other iron from the house of Ndaba.
Piercing pillar that spears the dying beam,
toughened leather rope of the amaNtandeni.

Cutter of good sticks among the thorns,
cutting down the dark paths of foolishness.
He visits all the corners of the earth;
he stirs and the world is stirred,
he who embraces the globe like a mythical creature,
he who swims the Vaal river,
he who drinks from the Zambezi –
he is the servant of the nations of Africa.

Ubakhonzil' abaMbo nabaNguni;
Wabakhonz' abeSuthu nabaTshwana;
Wawakhonz' amaZulu kaSenzangakhona;
Wawakhonz' amaSwazi namaNdebele;
Wawakhonz' amaTshona, amaNyasa namaKhalanga;
Wadib' izizw' ezikhulu nezincinane,
Edal' umanyano lwama-Afrika,
Ukuz' inimb' ibe nye yezizwe.

Yimbuzu-mbuz' enjengesinaliti,
Inzwan' enkulu yakwaMthikrakra;
Umbol' izizazobe into kaMandela.
Umafanelwa zidanga nezidabane;
Umafanelwa yimbol' engayiqabi,
Azi, ngekuyini na beth' eyiqaba?
Umagxagxamis' amagxagx' axhalabe,
Umaphongomis' izizwe ziphonyoze.

Aa! Zweliyashukuma!
Aa! Ndlela-zimhlophe kaMandela!
UZweliyashukum' elibizwa zizizwe;
UNdlela-zimhloph' elibizwa yimbongi;
Kub' udale kwamhloph' eAfrika;
Laphum' ilanga latshis' ooTshinga-liyatsha.
Baphutshuluk' ooBhakaqana ligqats' ezinkqayini;
Bagungquz' ooMgulukudu besoyik' imbuthu-mbuthu;
Baphongom' ooRheme betshelwe sicheko;
Zantantazel' iinyhwagi zibon' ukutsha kwelizwe.

Thetha, mfo kaMandela! Thetha, nkosi yam!
Theth' ungoyiki kusekh' impund' eAfrika!
Maz' ungaboyik' ooSiswana-sibomvana,

He serves the abaMbo and the amaNguni,
and he serves the Sotho and the Tswana;
and he serves the Zulu of Senzangakhona,
and he serves the Swazi and Ndebele,
and he serves the Shona, the Malawians and the Kalanga;
he criss-crosses nations, large and small,
creating unity among Africans,
all the nations sharing the pain of the birth of unity.

He pierces like a needle,
this handsome man of the house of Mthikrakra.
Ochre covers his chest, this son of Mandela:
he can wear the royal necklace and oribi cloak;
red ochre suits him, even though he does not wear it
– oh, what would he be if he wore it?
He who jolts the arrogant ones into apprehension;
he dismays them, rattles them and leaves them in disarray.

Hail! Earthquake!
Hail! Progress wrought by Mandela!
Other nations call you Earthquake;
the iimbongi call you: Shining-Open-Road,
because you let Africa shine.
The sun will rise and consume the scornful ones,
the careless ones will flee, the sun scorching their bald heads;
these clumsy ones will stumble around, cringing with fear;
their mouths will go dry;
like genets, they will scurry away from a thirsty land.

Speak up, son of Mandela! Speak, my chief!
Speak without fear, there are still survivors of the disaster in Africa!
Don't fear Those-with-the-Sunburnt-Bellies,

OoSobindeka nooQhinga-libhentsile.
Bonga bakubon' amadlala,
Kanti kukrakr' inyaniso;
Kuba kamb' ihlaba ngokwekhala,
Budul' ububhengeqa nobungqwangangqwili.

Thetha, mThemb', ungoyiki kusekh' amadoda!
Theth' ungoyiki kusekh' amadod' eAfrika!
Mhlawumbi la mathamb' angarhashaza,
Lith' ithambo libuyele kwithambo lalo;
Kub' uThix' uSomandl' uyalawula,
Uyawakhawulezis' amaxesh' akhe.
Ubhukuq' izikumkan' ezikhulu,
Aphakamis' izizwan' ezidelekileyo.

Thetha, kwedin' akwaZondw', ungoyiki!
Ungazoyik' iinyhwagi neembodla.
Nokufa kusakulindele,
Kwaye kusakulungele,
Ube lidini lesizwe sikaNtu,
Kub' ungumntwan' egazi ngendalo.
Wavelel' ukuthwal' ezo nzingo neenzima,
Ezinye nezinye phezu kwezinye.
Ngaman' uThixo wakusikelela,
Wakuphumeza, wakuthamsanqelisa,
Uboyis' ububi neent' ezimbi.
      Makube njalo, nkosi yam.

the ones who are choked with fervour, and have indecent plans.
They will see their flaws
and the truth will be bitter,
it will stab like aloe:
when you prick yourself on it, the pain is as bitter as exposing evil
    and malevolence.

Speak, Mthembu, do not fear!
Speak, there still are stalwarts in Africa!
Even the bones are stirring and making sounds;
every bone wants to return to its original place;
because God the Almighty reigns,
He will hasten his times,
He overturns great kingdoms
and elevates un-esteemed nations.

Speak, son of Zondwa, and do not fear
the spotted genets and the greedy
    caracals!
Death already awaits you,
but life fits you so fittingly,
you've become the sacrifice of the African nations,
you have true royalty in your blood.
You arrived to carry the suffering and oppression,
the one heaped upon the other.
May God bless you and let you succeed,
so that we triumph over evil and malevolence.
May it be like that for ever and ever.
    Let it be so, my Lord.

Translated from isiXhosa by Koos Oosthuysen and Gabeba Baderoon

Igama lephoyisa uSwanepuli

Mazisi Kunene

Kwenziwa yini njalo nxa ngilizwa igama lakho
Ngishaywe luvalo ngitatazele nasendlini
Ngivale amasango ngize ngiwavale nangensimbi?
Kwenziwa yini igama lakho libe njalo lingesinda
Ngize ngithi uma ngiphuma ngihlome?

The name of the policeman, Swanepoel

Mazisi Kunene

Why is it that whenever I hear your name,
I am struck by fear, agitated in my own house
even shutting the gates with the iron lock?
Why is it that your name is like that, so heavy on me
that when I go out I have to be armed?

Translated from isiZulu by Nkosinathi Sithole

Incwadi kaMandela kuNomzamo, esejele iminyaka engamashumi amabili nane

Mazisi Kunene

Selokhu ngabika kuwe sengibale iminwe emihlanu
Ngithe ngifika koweshumi nambili ngangisindana
Ngangivuvuke zozimbili izinyawo
Ngenxa yelizwi lakho ngabekezela
Ngazengatshatha imizimba eqaqambayo
Ngangingesiyimi sengifika kowekhulu
Ngasengihamba phakathi kwamaphupho
Ngasengimbona okunguyena umthumileyo
Ngimbona emi kude emaphesheya
Ngimuzwa nangezindlebe eshaya imitshingo
Ngangijamela kuye ngithi akaze asondele
Ngambona esekhomba izindlela
Ngamuzwa esengibeletha ngelizwi lakho
Ngathi sengiluqedile lonke uhambo
Ngaphenduka ngayibona imibono
Kwakunguwe usugoduka usumuhle kangakaya
Usuyifezile yonke imidanti yamaThongo akwethu.

Mandela's letter to Nomzamo (One-Who-Is-Tested-Beyond-Endurance), during the time he was in jail for twenty-four years

Mazisi Kunene

Since I reported to you, I have counted on five fingers,
when I reached the twelfth, I was borne down by heaviness,
both my feet were swollen.
Your voice made me continue
so I could carry bodies filled with pain on my back.
When I reached a hundred, I was no longer myself,
I was travelling in the midst of dreams.
Then I saw the one you had sent,
I saw her standing at a distance, on the other side,
my ears heard her playing the reedpipes,
I gazed at her, urging her to come closer,
I saw her pointing at the route,
I heard her carrying me on her back with your voice,
and so I could finish the journey,
I turned and saw visions:
it was you leaving; you were so beautiful,
having fulfilled all the desires of my ancestors.

Translated from isiZulu by Nkosinathi Sithole

Impophoma yeVictoria

BW Vilakazi

Gobhoza kuze kube nini manzi
Agubha ngempophoma nokwesaba,
Nobuhle! Yebo, ungaphazanyiswa
Gobhoza nokujul' okungaziwa!
UNkulunkul' ogcobe isimongo
Sekhanda lakho ngomudwa wothingo.
Lwenkosikazi, nenkung' engapheli
Egubuzele izinyawo zakho.
Ukuphe nezwi lokuqhaqhabuka,
Namandl' okukhuluma naye yedwa,
Laph' uthulis' imilomo yesintu
Ngaphezu kwedwala laseSibungu.

Mamo! Uban' ongas' asukumele
Phezul' answininize njengentethe
Yomhlabathi weshongololo ngoba
Ethemb' impikisano nawe Dumase?
Esuswa nhlungu zini naluthando
Lwakuxobisa ngamsindo muni?
Nolwandle luhoxekela emuva
Lusinel' emuva njengezomgqizo
Kunoba lwelanyathiselwe nawe;
Nkathimbe luyalala luthi daxa
Njengomunt' osedakwe wacobeka
Yilanga nawumsebenzi onzima.

Kunjal' ulwandle luyazikhathaza,
Ludunduzel' amagagas' emzansi,
Luwagogel' umhlambikazaluse,

The Victoria Falls

BW Vilakazi

Flow on forever, waters that roar
with fearful fury and splendour,
Beautiful One! Flow on undisturbed!
Flow with unknowable depth!
God anointed your forehead
with the colours of the rainbow.
The thunderous spray cloaking your feet,
He endowed you with a voice
that thunders,
and the power to commune with Him alone;
above the rock of Sibungu
you drown the voices of mere mortals.

Good heavens! For who, like a cricket that rolls around with
    songololos,
can be bold enough
to start shrieking shrilly
in a challenge to your roar, Great Thunderer?
Inspired by what miseries,
who can be bold enough to pester with what sounds?
Even the sea is on the retreat,
her waves pulling back
like rows of dancers at a contest;
and, rather than be compared with you,
she lies in repose,
like one drunk from too much toil and heat.

Yes, even the sea
ventures forth to curb the waves in anxiety,

Asin' imini nobusuk' engemi.
Ngeliny' ilang' abuy' adambe phansi,
Acweng' ubuhle besibhakabhaka.
Kwenziwa yini wena ungaphozi,
Ungagugeli phansi ugobhoza
Udwengula impophoma kaVictoria,
Ngeliny' ilang' ungadambeli phansi
Kodw' ugobhoz' imini nobusuku?
Yeka lokhu kukhuthala okungaka!

Kaning' ikhwezi likaMhlayonke
Seloku lavul' amehlo phezulu,
Lakuzwa ububula njengempisi.
Nezinkanyezi zesibhakabhaka
Ezikhanyise zilind' imini
Yomyalo wengelosi laph' umhlaba
Uyakudazuluk' uncibilike,
Uvulekele phezu kukaThixo,
Namehlo akh' ahlaba njengomkhonto
Zibek' indlebe phezu kwezwi lakho
Dumase, ngathi zithi: "Hamba njalo
Wen' ovalelis' ungavalelisi."

Ihlamvu lonk' eliphukazelela
Lengamel' iziziba zakho zonke,
Lidonsa lonk' uhlaza lwemithambo
Esegazini lal' eziphethwini
Zemijobulukana yamandambi
Apheshethwa ngumoya wenyakatho.
Bheka-ke, naz' inyoni zindizela
Zizimis' isibindi zisondela
Eduze, zibhukudis' izimpaphe

not unlike a shepherd
who gathers his flock so they may not stray.
Some days, the waters are tranquil,
mirroring the splendour of the sky.
Why is it you never pause,
eternally filling the chasms below
with your roar, oh Victoria,
why not pause for one day
your thundering by day and by night?
Such industriousness!

Countless times the morning star,
since it first blessed the skies with its smile,
has heard you growl like a hyena.
The stars of the sky,
huddled together like sentinels,
wait patiently for the earth to crumble,
as foretold by an angel;
then you'll be restored before God's eyes,
which pierce like a spear.
The stars listen to your voice,
Great Thunderer, as if saying, "Flow on,
You who are always threatening departure, but never departs!"

There are tree branches hanging
over your lakes,
the roots sucking sustenance from your springs
and rains thrown by the northern winds
that rage through boiling channels and gorges below.
Behold the birds swirling in circles,
unperturbed by your roar
as they bathe their wings

Phakathi kofasimbe nay' inkungu
Oyiphefumulela ngaphezulu!
Kazinayo nangebhe yalo msindo.

Kuyinjabulo ngisho ukuthinta
Umphetho weminyibe yesibhamba
Esingamful' ukhalo lweVictoria
Laph' imichilo yemvul' eyehlayo
Ixoshan' ishayek' edwaleni,
Kuqhume imiqhele yamagwebu,
Kudamuzeke nentuthu yamanzi
Eyona ifihla imingcwi yamaza,
Iveza nothingo lwenkosikazi
Oluyinhlobisalanga emini.
Iyona l' eyakh' umthal' ebusuku,
Iwufafaza ngezinkwenkwezana.

Min' engingenal' izwi njengelakho
EIokhu limi njalo limpompoza,
Kunjengomfanekiso wesilima
Uma ngiling' ukuchaza phansi
Ngalolu sib' olugcobhoz' uyinki
Isimo sobukhosi nesobuhle –
Ngenzela nokuvus' uthando kubo
Abangazange bakubone ngeso.
Uphumuz' imiphefumul' ehlwelwe,
Eyimihambima ingenandawo
Yokubeka nohlangothi ngenkathi
Ilizw' elakho izwi ikubheka.

Amehlo abo agcwal' intokozo,
Bahlale phansi bazicobelele

in the torrential spray –
here's the mist
that you breathe into the atmosphere.

How joyous to touch the hem of the waistcloth
that hugs Victoria's waist,
where streamers of rain cascade
to strike the rocks below,
exploding into perpetual sprays:
crowns of foam
and shimmering rainbows
and incandescent sunbeams.
Night and day a Milky Way
with its silvery light
pockmarks the sky
with starlets that glitter
in the atmosphere.

I, whose voice is not potent enough
to match your untiring roar,
must seem like a buffoon
as I, with my quill and ink,
attempt to capture in words
your awesome majesty and splendour –
it's just a lame attempt at inspiring
those who have yet to look on your beauty.
You offer a sanctuary to those ambushed
by nightfall in the wilderness,
the strayed and forlorn, the destitute and despondent
who can only take refuge in the roar of your voice,
the magnificence of your appearance.

Insangu, bashay' amadosh' ogwayi,
Babheme bakubuke baze bome
Bomel' ubuthongo bazilalele.
Umsindo wakh' unjengoju lwenyosi,
Unjengesandla somzanyan' ekhanda,
Selul' iminwe sithungath' unwele
Silulalisa, siluvusa phansi.
Nemihambim' ithol' isiphephelo
Ngasezimpikweni zamanz' amhlophe
Adilika empophomeni yakho.
Dilika njal' uzubikele bonke
Abenzalo ye-Afrik' abezayo!

How their eyes glow with joy,
as they sit relaxed
to share dagga pipes, tip tins of snuff.
They stare hungrily at you
until sleep conquers them.
Your roar is sweet as honey,
soft and tender as a nurse's comforting caress,
her fingers tracing patterns on a destitute's head,
paying astute attention to each strand of hair.
The wanderers find refuge in this way
under the white wings
of your torrential waters.
Cascade forever, sound a clarion call
to generations still to come from Africa!

Translated from isiZulu by Fred Khumalo

Mohokare (Caledon river)

KE Ntsane

Harehare, setsing sa Maloti,
BoPhofong, melokoloko ea dithaba,
Ntho tsa ho hlaba mokgosi
Ha tshweu ya maru e atametse,
Ke hona moo o tswang teng,
Mophekapheka towe wa noka,
Ba o tsebang ba reng o Mohokare.

Mohloding wa hao ho a tshabeha;
Ekare ho phela teng kganyapahadi,
Ntho a ho kwenya dikgomo le batho!
Ba o bonang ba sa tsebe ha enomoholo,
Ba ka qaputsa metsing a hao ka sebete,
Ba sa tsebe hoba ha enomoholo ho a tshabeha,
Ba kileng ba nyarela teng, mmele e a baleha,
Ba re ba bone dihele hantle!

Ka mona ka Kapa, dinoka le dinokana dia lla,
Hoba metsi a pjhele, di omme,
Empa wena, molollope o mpa di kgolo,
Ha ho mohla o robalang o itsosa,
Hoba mmao ke mosadi a Letebele, o a sisa,
Fubeng sa hae ho nyantse banna,
Tsona kwankwetla tsena: BoSenqu,
BoLethuela le ba bang boramohlongwana;
Re sa bale tshenyane ena ya boSemena.

Ha o hwasa jwalo, Ntsho Tala,
O tsamaya o dikela ka ena kgohlo,

Mohokare, place of the willows

KE Ntsane

Deep, deep within the Maluti mountains,
high on Mont-Aux-Sources where snow sifts like flour,
where alarms sound,
when the white of clouds approaches,
it is there that you originate,
you, Reptile-That-Is-a-Big-Snake,
those who know you call you Mohokare.

There where you begin, things are terrifying:
it looks as if an enormous water snake lives there,
a thing that could swallow cattle and people!
Those who see you, not knowing your origin,
paddle bravely with oars in your water,
oblivious of the terror at your source,
those who glimpsed it, their bodies ran away,
they say they have seen the embodiment of hell!

In the Cape, rivers and rivulets are crying,
the waters have dried up, so they are dry,
but you, Long-One-with-the-Big-Stomach,
there is not a day that you sleep or wake up hungry.
Your mother is an Ndebele whose milk flows in easy abundance,
at her breast many men have suckled,
strong men such as the Senqu river and its tributaries:
the Tugela and tributaries and other chiefs;
not counting maggot-like rivulets such as the Semena.

As we hear you thundering, Black-Green One,
walking and disappearing down this gorge,

O hopotse kae re tsebe, leha re ke ke ra tseka?
Na ha o bone o siya mahlomola morao?
Ba heno ba tla utlwa bohloko,
Ha baditjhaba ba o tsholela maqa,
Ba re o a ikgantsha, o Letebele,
O ba hohola feela ba se na molato?

Dumela, moraparapa tooe o matswedintsweke,
Wena lewatle la Maburu le Basotho,
Le hoja ba sa buisane hantle pela hao.
Hoba hola Majoro a se o bone,
Makeleketla e ka be le ha 'Mmantšebo hantle.
O buile Mosotho a kgale, mo-lula-kgotla,
A re: "Se-ja-monna ha se mo qete."

O lelemela, o ya kae, ntho towe,
O sehang naha tsa Makgowa ka lehare?
Ba bang ba re o ya Borwa,
Athe nna ke a tseba hoba o ramethinya,
O tla hwasa jwalo, o thetse matlaopa,
A nna re o nkgile wa Borwa;
Athe o habile lewatleng, Bophirimela;
Hoba e moholo o sa o eteletse pele.

Nka o bolela ka reng, Mohokare?
Pina tsa hao ha o theosa dikgohlo,
Ke bo-koli-ya-malla, pakamahlomola,
Pina tsa ho lahlisa Mosotho mmae,
Melodi e ratwang ke Makgowa sehloho.
O theosa jwalo o tjodietsa sa ngwana lela,
Ere o feta Kgoro-e-betlwa,
O bo ngotlile mohwasa, o ka leshodu!

where are you off to, we have to know though we may not argue?
Don't you see that you leave grief in your wake?
The people of your place will be hurt
when other nations throw bad words at you,
saying that you behave arrogantly like an Ndebele,
you sweep people away without reason.

Hail and be hailed, you big writhing reptile!
You are the sea between Boer and Basotho,
although they do not speak well to one another when near you.
If Major Warden had not seen you,
then Winburg would have belonged to Mantshebo fully.
The old Mosotho spoke well; vigilant in the council,
he said, "We will recover what we have lost."

Where are you flowing to, you scoundrel,
you who cut the farms of the whites right in the middle?
Some suggest you are flowing south,
but I know that you are the father of pretending,
you will thunder and frighten the stupid ones,
they will think you are flowing south;
but you are on your way to the sea in the west;
because the Big One has already gone ahead of you.

How can I praise you, Mohokare?
Your songs when you meander through the ravines
are laments, evidence of great sorrow,
the songs that saw a Mosotho part from his mother,
yet these melodies were loved by the whites.
You flow away weeping like a child who weeps,
but when you flow past Kgoro-e-betlwa,
you flow quietly as a thief!

Mmamahohoretsane towe, Mohokare!
O tsamayang o hohola medidima difate,
O tlosa tlhapi tulong tsa yona,
O nka Mosotho a tshela Frei Stata,
O mo hlabise hlohlodingwane;
Buru o le hlobodise dijase, le kgolokgothehe!
O shwele pelo keng o le motsamai,
O ratang ho inea leona ka bana ba batho?

Molato, le teng, hase wa hao,
Hoba lewatle le o laetse jwalo,
La re o hohole le bona bo-tsipa-sehole.
Jwale o so le ramelato-ha-efele,
Hoba le moreneng ha o sa shejwa,
Batho e se le boSenqu, ba nang le mabitso,
Leha ho le jwalo, Basotho le Maburu ba o roka,
Ba re wa ba thusa, wa ba etsetsa moedi!

Nka tshela Mohokare, ka baka mahlomola,
Ka siya mme le ntate, ka ya ditjhabeng,
Hona kwana bitleng la bana ba Mohato.
Ngwana ha tshela Mohokare pelo e a senyeha,
A hopola tsa mehleng ya bontate,
Ha ba sa ntsane ba tsekisana naha.
Lelemela, o hwase sedutse, putswabodiba,
O yo kena ho Senqu, o ntsa o emetse,
Bedi ba lona le ise tshila tsa rona lewatleng,
Re sale re le basweu ho feta lehlwa.

You who gathers everything, Mohokare!
You, flowing, sweep big trees with you,
you, flowing, sweep fish from their homes,
you, flowing, sweep the Mosotho crossing from the Free State,
you make him somersault;
you rip the coat from a Boer and let him run!
You are ruthless while you are travelling,
you love being blamed for ill-treating humanity.

Guilt is not yours,
because the sea has instructed you
to sweep away those who ignore the calls of the chief.
Now you are the father of never-ending problems,
because even the king now despises you,
Senqu-and-them are the ones who are famous,
but even so, the Basotho and Boers praise you,
they say you helped them, you made a border for them!

When I crossed the Mohokare, I created sadness,
left my mother and father behind and joined the strangers,
over on that side with them are the graves of Mohato's children.
If a child crosses the Mohokare, his heart becomes wounded,
he thinks about the times of the ancestors,
when they fought to keep their land.
Flow quickly and rustle gently, you Grey-One-of-the-Deep-Pools,
go and flow into the Senqu who is waiting for you,
both of you wash our impurities down into the sea,
and leave us behind, purer than snow.

Translated from Sesotho by Tšepiso Samuel Mothibi and
Johannes Lenake

Ukufa

LMS Ngcwabe

(Ah! Ngqonge-ngqongendini kaQubul'egqitha!!!)

Ho-o-o-o-o-o-o-oyina!
Thambo-dala kade bemqongqotha!
Diza-dala kade bemkhwahlaza!
Wen' ukad' ukhonkothwa zizinja!
Wen' ukad' unethwa naziimvula!
    Gqala lamagqala,
    Tshawe lamatshawe,
    Kufandin', akufi!

Kwakudala-dala, kwamhla-mnene,
Kwamandulo phaya entlandlolo
Wawusel' ukad' ququzela.
Gqogq' eqhuqha, nqwelo yogoduko!
    Choph' emanxebeni,
    Xhaph' axel' ixhwili,
    Ntondini-ndini!

Nyokandini emakhanda-khanda!
Nkunz' abayikhuz ingekahlabi!
Gila-ngophondo ngabula bhejana!
Beth' ebuya, zulu laseMthatha!
    Mdali weenkedama,
    Mthombo weenyembezi,
    Chibi lokuncama!

Lifukazi eligqum' umhlaba,
Wen' uphaphazela emoyeni,
Wen' udada emanzin' olwandle,

Death

LMS Ngcwabe

(Oh! You-Who-Unexpectedly-Arrives, Difficult-One-Who-
   Always-Surrounds-Us)

Ho-o-o-o-o-o-o-oyina!!! Listen to me!
Old bone whose marrow has long been knocked out!
Old mealie stalk stripped long ago of its corn!
You whom the dogs have long barked at!
You whom the rain rains upon, as hardened as an old soldier!
    Oldest of the old!
    Sovereign of sovereigns!
    Death, you cannot die!

Long long ago, in the distant past,
in the old days, in times long gone,
you were already busy.
Clip-clop, clip-clop, you wagon of those going home!
    You crouch next to the wounded,
      licking up the blood like a wild dog,
      you thing of all things!

You Head-Headed Snake!
You bull whom people fear even before you gore,
battering with your horn like a rhinoceros,
thundering like the weather of Mthatha!
    Creator of orphans,
    fountain of tears!
    Hippo-pool of desperation!

Great cloud that covers the earth!
You who flies through the air!

Wen' uzula-zul' emahlathini,
Wen' ugush' ingcwaba,
Wen' unxib' iintsizi,
Wen' uthwel' iintlungu!

Wen' ungena phi naphi naphi na,
Wen' uhlinza-hlinza njalo-njalo,
Ndutyumbana yesirhovu-rhovu,
Gelekeqe-geqe, geqe, geqe!
    Ginyi, ginyi, ginyi;
    Ginyi, ginyi, ginyi;
    Ginyi, ginyi, ginyi!

Lemb' igqirh' iingcambu zathi shwaka.
Yayikhul' incwina egumbini.
Yayingen' iphum' ihlunguzela
Imilowo kwanamagqoboka.
    Kwaneenyembezi
    Azafeza lutho.
    Kuf', akunanceba!

Bendisithi wakha wathandazwa;
Bendisithi wakha walulekwa;
Bendisithi wakha wakhalinywa;
Ngathi nkqu noYesu wamoyisa.
    Kufandin', akuva;
    Kufandin', akufi;
    Kufa, uneenkani!

Ho-o-o-o-o-o-o-oyina!
Ndandihlala ndithi ndiya kwazi;
Ndandihlala ndithi uya ndazi;

You who swims in the sea!
You who criss-crosses the bush!
>You conceal the grave!
>You clothe yourself in mourning!
>You bear the ultimate pain!

You spread here and there and everywhere.
You go on slaughtering and slaughtering.
You gangster continuously gorging yourself!
You gobbling glutton greedily guzzling!
>Swallowing, swallowing, swallowing.
>Swallowing, swallowing, swallowing.
>Swallowing, swallowing, swallowing.

The traditional healer digs for roots until nothing is left.
The volume of the lament swells in the room.
It swells and fades in sympathy
with both the relatives and the converts.
>The flood of tears
>achieves nothing.
>Death, you have no mercy!

It seems that people tried to change you through prayer.
It seems that people tried to educate you.
It seems that people tried to argue with you.
But you even seem to have defeated Jesus.
>Death, you do not hear.
>Death, you do not die.
>Death, you are the essence of stubbornness!

Listen to me-e-e-e!
I kept on saying that I knew you.

Kunamhlanje uyandongamela;
Kunamhlanje uxing' emqaleni;
   Kunamhlanj' ingqondo
   Iyarhawuzela.
   Zwindin', uphi na?

Zizipotsololo zabafana
Ezo mbalasane zomlisela
Namagqabikaz' eziponono.
Ezo mbalasane zomthinjana
   Azibanga dini
   Likwanelisayo,
   Mqala-mde kaXesha!

Ntomb' emnyam' enqunyulw' amabele,
Kant' iza kuncancis' uhodoshe.
Ganda-gand' ongath' unyumbaziwe,
Kant' ufunzele esihogweni.
   Nozihelegushe,
   Nomathwabendini,
   Nontlekelendwane!

Cikokazi leminyaka-nyaka,
Ntak' evum' ingom' elalisayo
Ubuthongo obungapheliyo,
None, none, none, none, none!
   Nzim, nzim, nzim!
   Cimi, cimi, cimi!
   Zole, cwaka, tu!

I kept on thinking that you knew me.
But until today you overwhelm me.
Until today you stick in my throat.
> Up to today my mind
> scratches around.
> Word, where are you?

All the handsome young men
and the famous men,
all the beautiful young women,
and the famous women,
> were not a sacrifice
> big enough for you,
> you, the long greedy throat of Time!

A black woman whose breasts have been cut off,
you see to it that she suckles greenbottles.
You grind your way like a road-grader,
but you yourself will end up in hell.
> Pleading is futile.
> Death rattling in your throat,
> it is all a disaster.

For years and years you've been the eloquent one,
like a bird singing people to sleep,
a sleep that never ends.
Their eyelids close, close, close, close, close!
> A lamp darkens, darkens, darkens!
> Quiet, tranquillity, end!
> Stillness, silence, nothing!

Translated from isiXhosa by Koos Oosthuysen and Gabeba Baderoon

Polokong (ya mokgalabje yo e bego e le molemi)

Moses Bopape and Stephen Ratlabala

Bjale lefase, re go nea mokgomana ye,
Yo le bego le gwerane kudu.
Robatša mmele wa gagwe o o lapilego,
Mo mobung wa gago, wo
A bego a o tseba gabotse,
Ga a sa tšhaba leswiswi le go tonya,
O tla no itulela le dipeu tše yena
Ka noši a di bjetšego.

Funeral (of an old man who was a farmer)

Moses Bopape and Stephen Ratlabala

Now dear earth, we give to you this esteemed elder,
who was your beloved friend.
Let sleep this body that is so tired,
here in you, earth,
that he knew so well.
He is no longer afraid of the dark and the cold,
he will go and sit by the seed
that he planted all by himself.

Translated from Sepedi by
Antjie Krog, supported by PS Groenewald's Afrikaans translation

Laboraro le lesoleso

HML Lentsoane

A kwagetše phirimana' Labobedi mabarebare,

A tswalela mantho tlabego,

Ntlha le thito ya ba koma.

E gorogile melaetša ka kgonono,

E hlatšwa ke thomo ya semuma,

Thomo ya go hloka matepe.

E tsitsinketšwe thomo,

Ya fetlekwa ka lepopodumo,

Ya ahlaahlwa ka megopolo ya lenyatšo,

Mafelelong ya fegwa,

Kgauswi ya ba kgweranong le badimo.

Ba tlorotše ditsebe boMmakhulwane,

Melomo ya tswalana le megala,

Ditsebe le tšona tša gana go hlaolwa.

Di feafeile maswiswing ditšhatšha,

Tša kopanya boTedukhulwana.

Mahlo a phadimile nke ba seetšwe,

Boroko gwa robalwa go pontšwe ka ihlo le tee.

A foile mathapisana a maso,

A fula dingwe di robetše.

A iswaiswile mpeng ya bošego,

A fetša ka go bonela mahube a banna.

Le hlabile la hloka matepe,

La hlaba leo le bego le letetšwe,

La hlatloga ka ntle le mathaithai.

A be a ragetše maswiswi ntlong maakabosane,

A phatlalala le metsemeso,

A ipala ka magorogoro.

Polelo a boletše ya go tsebja ke beng,

Black Wednesday

HML Lentsoane

The rumours were already circulating on that Tuesday evening,
they left people astonished,
though the real truth remained a mystery.
Messages were received with scepticism,
they were vomited by the newspapers,
the faithful messengers.
Eyes were glued to the newspapers,
they were analysed with disbelief,
then they received attention from Those-Who-Express-Loudly-
 Their-Thoughts-of-Scorn.
Eventually that was put in abeyance.
We were on the brink of death; the time for the covenant of the
 forefathers had come.
The Blood-spillers pricked up their ears,
their mouths befriended telephones,
their ears refused to be left in the dark.
Experts worked through the night;
they gathered Those-with-Red-Beards.
Their eyes looked bruised, glittered as if invaded by rumours,
they slept with one eye closed.
They became aware of a coming darkness,
they grazed while others were asleep.
Those-with-Red-Beards worked tirelessly in the middle of the night,
they worked until the early hours of the morning.
The sun rose with no sign of the calamity,
then the day arrived that everyone had been waiting for,
it rose well without any cunning.
Darkness was driven towards the locust-birds,
the Red-Beards spread themselves throughout the townships,

Polelo ya go bolelwa ke mašela,

Polelo ya go bolelwa ke dipampiri,

Polelo ya go bolelwa o rokile molomo.

Le hlatlogile la hloka matepe,

La rotoga le khoše dithopa.

Khudu e phulegile legapi ka sekgalela,

Gwa šala go nkga go sa bola,

Monkgo wa tlapela gohle.

La bogologolo le sobetše ka sekgalela,

Gwa hlaba le lefsa ka bonako.

Baleng le badikeng ntšu la lehlabula e bile le tee.

Dipampiridillo di tšholotše megokgo,

Tša goeletša di homotše,

Tša rafolla tša mafahleng,

Tša se dikadike le gatee.

Mošito go kwetše o tee,

Koša gwa gobja ya go loya,

Ya go hlogohla batheeletši maikutlo.

Moya go nkgile wa bonaba,

Gwa tšutla wa go emaemiša meriri.

Metato e batile mantho ditsebe,

Difatanaga tša ya tlase le tletlolo.

Sibi le Mole di hlakahlakane le koma,

Tša hloka hlong,

Tša hlomarana le babolodi.

Moretlwa go hwidintšwe wa molongwanamoswana,

O kidimetša, o rotoga go rakoporo,

O šišinya naga yohle.

Go senyegile le eja motho,

Gwa nkga nama' motho mosegare wo monana.

E ganne go bona mathata a loya koma,

Polelo ya bolela ye mpsha manthong.

they gathered themselves in various groups.

As for language, they used the one known to them,

the language of the cloth,

the language spoken by documents,

the language spoken with the mouth sewn shut.

The sun soared without any sign of the calamity,

it moved saturated with secrets.

That day, at midday, the tortoise-shell burst open,

the situation turned ugly,

the smell defiled everything.

The sun eclipsed during daytime, as it once did, long ago,

a new sun rose.

The male and female initiates united with one voice.

Petitions were handed over,

the newspapers shouted silently,

they revealed the concerns of their chests,

they did not beat about the bush.

One rhythm was heard,

the chant became mesmerising,

it shook everybody's understanding.

There was an atmosphere of rivalry,

a strong wind was blowing.

Telephones were mounted on human ears,

vehicles moved up and down.

Sibi and Mole, the spies, were seen amongst the initiates,

they were unashamed,

they betrayed the initiates.

Assegais-with-Small-Dark-Mouths – rifles – were used,

heavy gun-sounds boomed from those wearing helmets,

the sounds shattered the whole country.

Pandemonium ensued at midday:

the smell of human flesh was everywhere.

Polelo e boletše ya mankgwari,

Hlaga ya aparela mašemo a kgauswi,

Gwa šala go nkga pilo fela.

Volkswagen e hlabile matshomane e ponapona,

Ford ya šala e sekame ka lehlakore,

Bedford e hloname, e llwe ke hlaga.

Bengmašemo ba se kgitlile,

Ya ba ge ba lebeletše marapo fela.

Leratadima le kgabišitšwe ke meši ye meso,

La tšea sefoka ka moyamoethimodišo,

Motho a šala a lla sehlodimare.

Nonyanatshipi e fofafofile sebakabekeng,

E omaoma e sa kotame,

E hlapeditše mathata' letšatši,

Moya e re hemiša wo mokoto,

E re khoriša wa go galaka,

Moya' go se phediše.

Metseng go tswakatswakane,

Gwa se be motšofadi,

Gwa se be segotlane.

Tše khulong di botogile di thuntša marole.

Di penne mesela bokadiphepheng,

Di tlopatlopišwa ke tlalelo.

Ditimela di hlakane hlogo,

Tša se tsebe ntlha le thito,

Tša fetša ka go khutša sebakanyana.

Le fefile la leba bothateng,

La ukamela madibeng a masomaso.

E phutšwe methopo ya madi,

Ya šala e re thapathapa!

Ya šala e huba bokadinoka.

Ba maatla ba bolaile,

The pandemonium worsened when people realised the hardship
   befalling the initiates,
a new language was used in speaking to the people.
The language used was that of fire;
this extended to the neighbouring villages:
what remained were ashes.
A Volkswagen squatted nakedly in the fire,
then a Ford went to lie on its side,
a Bedford was burned to ashes.
The owners were visibly upset,
weeping while gazing at the charred bones.
The sky was adorned with thick black smoke,
tufts of tail exploded with Air-That-Makes-One-Sneeze,
people were left crying helplessly.
A small iron bird tilted to and fro in the sky,
it hovered but never sat down,
it kept vigil, controlling the day's riots,
it made us inhale a thick wind,
it left us with a bitter taste,
a deadly smoke.
Pandemonium was the order of the day in the communities,
the elderly were not distinguishable,
the babies were not distinguishable.
The big bulls, the armoured tanks, turned hastily and kicked up
   dust.
Their tails scorpion-like in the air,
they hop-hopped howling from distress.
The trains were confused,
they were unsure how to manoeuvre,
and decided to retire.
Eventually the sun set,
it overlooked the deep and dark wells.

Metekatekana ya no swaišwa.

Meago e latswitšwe ke mollo,

Ya šala e ponapona.

Mello e tlapetše naga,

E amogela moengmofsa tlhokaleina,

E keka bošego le mosegare,

E metša bao e ba lebanego.

Bookelong ditšhaba di tsene di kgonne senko,

Baragwanath ya fetoga lewatle la megokgo,

Ya fetoga lewatle la madi.

Di okilwe dikgobadi,

Dikgobadi tša madimabe,

Dikgobadi tša go hloka molato,

Dikgobadi tša go emela therešo.

Di kgotleletše, tša menekana,

Mafelelong tša hwela therešo.

Atla tša madi di emetše kgole,

Tša thatafiša dipelo.

Taba ga e lale.

Dikuranta di ahlaahlile tiragalo tša letšatši,

Tša ala madireng ka botlalo,

Tša ntšha diswantšho tše bohloko,

Tša kgotla maikutlo a batswadi,

Tša ba tša tširoša le dikgope le mafetwa.

Diyalemoya di katane,

Tša bea mašabašaba seetšeng.

A tsene gare mabarebare,

Gwa se hlwe go tsebja nnete.

Badimo bešo, ke a le leboga,

Ke leboga ge le mphile maatla,

Le mpontšhitše tše tša Laboraro le.

Ke bone ka a ka mahlo,

Blood vessels had been cut,
blood was left gushing from the wounds!
It flooded heavily like hissing rivers.
The powerful had killed,
the youth were dead.
Buildings were burned,
they were left naked.
Fire overran the country,
becoming a new nameless visitor,
spreading day and night,
swallowing the righteous ones.
The hospital was filled with distressed people,
Baragwanath turned into a sea of tears,
it turned into a sea of blood.
The injured had been stabilised,
the unfortunate victims,
the blameless victims,
those who stood for truth.
They persevered, and writhed in pain:
in the end, they died for truth.
Those with bloody hands had disappeared;
they hardened their hearts.
This story will not go unreported.
The newspapers splashed the events of the day,
spread them fully everywhere,
they showed frightening pictures,
they disturbed the feelings of parents,
they touched the hearts of the unmarried.
The radios screamed,
they informed the nation.
The newspapers and radio were intermingled with rumour and
  hearsay,

Le ge a fokola, monagano ga o bjalo.

Ke thomile nke ke a lora

Kganthe ke hlatsa therešo ya poo.

Tša mosegare di ntlhobaeditše,

Ke re ke ikgakantšha tšona gwa pala.

Ke lekile go itebatša gwa gana,

Badimo ba re ke botše lefase tšeo ke di bonego.

Ga ke nyake go šupša ka menwana bosasa,

Ga ke nyake go ba sejato,

Ke nyaka go ithobalela ka khutšo bosasa.

Lefase, ke tšeo tša Laboraro le lesoleso Soweto.

Nka se di lebale tša June 16, 1976.

almost overshadowing the truth.

My ancestors, I am thankful to you,

thank you for giving me the strength,

you made it possible for me to witness the events of this Wednesday.

I saw them with my naked eyes:

although my eyes were weak, my mind was alert.

When it started, I thought I was dreaming,

only to discover that I was vomiting deep emotions.

The day's events left me depressed,

I tried in vain to ignore them.

I tried to forget them, but failed,

the ancestors directed me to share with the world what I saw.

I do not want to be blamed tomorrow,

I do not want to keep the memories only to myself,

I wish to die in peace one day.

Oh world, these were the events of that black Wednesday in Soweto.

I shall never forget the events of 16 June 1976.

Translated from Sepedi by Biki Lepota

Pula

LD Raditladi

Kgomo ya ga rre e lela kwa tennyanateng,
E letse malatsi a le mantsi digobo,
E bile mašwi a yone a tletse dithobeng,
E duma e se na epe pelo ya ditshebo.
Kodu ya yone e folotsha banna dikobo,
Ba tsene dikobong tsa tsatsi le penne,
Gore ba e utlwe e lela gararo le gane.

Kgomo ya ga rre ke raya maru a legodimo,
Ke raya maru a mantsho a mmala wa sebilo,
Tshephe naana e kgabaganya legodimo,
Jaaka dikanono ga e na botshabelo,
Ke tlhobolo tsa mmokofete molelo,
Tse di dumang thata di okame Leruti,
Mangolwane di mo pegile meriti.

Ya ipopa le loapi ya ikisa godimo,
Ya tshelaganya legodimo gantsintsi,
Ngwalenkolo a roromisa melomo,
A kgalema sebadimo ba le bantsi,
Metsi loaping a fologa jaaka dintsi,
Maru legodimong a nyera a ba a rotha,
Metsi a wela fa fatshe leratharatha.

Molebeledi wa kgomo tsa ga rara,
Tsa ga rara mararaanya letlhakola,
Mararaanya letlhakola pula e tsora,
Ke pula ya medupe e bolokang fela,
E fetolang lefatshe mebalabala,

Rain

LD Raditladi

The cow of my father lows from voluptuous fields,
for a few days she hasn't come home,
her milk burns her,
ceaselessly she lows.
The sound of her lowing wakens the men from their blankets,
those who sleep during the day
hear her continuous lowing.

If I talk about the cow of my father,
I am talking about clouds,
I am talking about dark, black, bundling clouds.
Look, the klipspringer flashes through the sky;
it is like a cannon that you cannot dodge,
and the firing guns echo across the Leruti mountains;
on Mangolwane mountain shadows fall.

The rain lifts herself up into the air and swells,
lightning carves busily to and fro,
the lips of the ancestors tremble with fury,
then they all thunder together like one,
and then the rain rustles in the sky like flies,
the clouds melt into one another and slink away,
big drops clatter leratha-ratha on the ground.

My father's cattle herder
knows very well that his cattle
graze in the bare gwarrie bush,
which, from the rain, becomes fecund and overgrown.
The soft rain resurrects everything,

E reng e tla go itlotlege digogwane,
Di goe ka di ne di ka dika di manne.

Pula mothusi wa dikhutsana tse dinnye,
Mothusi wa batho, namane ya legodimo,
Le segara mogatla e re fa se e bonye
Se lokoege jaaka theko ya lerumo,
Mmato a kwena o rale bodiba godimo,
Lefatshe lena le nne bophalaphala,
Nageng ditlhare o bone di tetesela.

the drizzle colours the sky in many colours,
even the frogs swell up and burst with sound.

Rain is the guardian of small stock, wild and tame,
rain is the guardian of humans,
it calves clouds making everything newborn and gleaming;
even those living tail between the legs – their tails like assegais
    shoot up straight,
and the upper body of the crocodile suddenly appears, crossing to
    new pools:
the earth is one big marsh upon marsh;
on the plains, from side to side, the trees are shimmering.

Translated from Setswana by Stephen Masote and Antjie Krog

About the poets

David Cranmer Theko Bereng (1905–1973)

Bereng was born in 1905, the son of Bereng Letsie and grandson of Letsie I, and a descendant of King Moshoeshoe I of Lesotho. He filled a number of positions during his life, serving as a member of the National Assembly of Basotholand and as acting king in the place of Theko Makhaola. He also served in the military in the Second World War. His only collection of poetry was published in 1931, entitled *Lithothokiso tsa Moshoeshoe le tse Ling* (The Poems of Moshoeshoe and Others). This was the first Sesotho poetry collection to be published, and although he only published this one collection, his influence as a Basotho poet was great. The poems are written in the traditional style of Sesotho praise poetry and centre on King Moshoeshoe I, whom Bereng saw as a symbol of Lesotho's greatness.

Moses Bopape

He is the author of *Ithute Direto*, in Sepedi, with Stephen Ratlabala.

James James Ranisi Jolobe (1902–1976)

Jolobe was born in 1902 in the Eastern Cape. Jolobe was well known as an author of isiXhosa fiction, poetry, and essays. His first novel, *uZagula*, was published in 1923. It was followed in 1928 by a number of poems published in an isiXhosa poetry anthology. He was also involved with the translation of literary works into isiXhosa, including Aesop's Fables (*Iintsomi zikaAesop*) and King Solomon's Mines (*Imigodi kaKumkani uSolomon*). Jolobe received three awards for his work, the May Ester Bedford Prize (1936), the Memorial Prize for Nguni literature (1952), and the Margaret Wrong Award (1953). He was also awarded an honorary doctorate from the University of Fort Hare for his work in editing an isiXhosa dictionary.

Bennett Makalo Khaketla (1913–2000)

Khaketla was born in Lesotho in 1913. He started out teaching at a number of schools around Lesotho and South Africa, and later became an influential Sesotho writer, publishing two novels and a number of plays and poems. He is known for his part in creating *Mohlabani* (Warrior), a popular newspaper in 1950s Lesotho, where he displayed his knowledge of international politics and documented the course of political change in that country. He became involved in politics and was a member of the Lesotho government.

Moabi S Kitchin (1907–?) and Neo H Kitchin (1909–?)

Very little is known about the Kitchin brothers. Both were born in Motito near Vryburg, North West Province and studied teaching at Tiger Kloof Educational Institution. They published a collection of Setswana poetry together with JM Lekgetho, titled *Boswa jwa Puo* (Legacy of the Language). Although they published their work in a single volume, each poem was credited to an individual author.

Mazisi Raymond Kunene (1930–2006)

Kunene, born in Durban, KwaZulu–Natal, was a distinguished poet, author and anti-apartheid activist. His talent for poetry and story-writing was recognised early on, with some of his work published in local newspapers by the time he was eleven. Kunene was exiled from South Africa in 1959 for opposing the apartheid government. Many of Kunene's works were originally written in isiZulu and later translated into English, his famous poem *Emperor Shaka the Great* among them. Kunene returned to South Africa in 1992. In 1993, he was made Africa's first poet laureate by the United Nations Educational, Scientific and Cultural Organisation in 1993, becoming South Africa's first poet laureate in 2005.

Ernest Pelaelo Lekhela (1913–1998)

Lekhela was born in Kimberley in 1913 where he attended St Matthews Anglican Mission School, Lyndhurst Road Public School, and CEC Mission Practising School. Lekhela dedicated his life to the academic community. Educator, musician, businessperson, and sports administrator, he had an impact on many fields. After serving as lecturer and then professor at the University of the North (now the University of Limpopo), he became the first vice-chair of the first Council of Universities of Bophuthatswana. Lekhela passed away in 1998 leaving behind numerous academic articles, a novel, and a book of poetry written in his home language, Setswana.

Herbert Mokadi Lucky Lentsoane (1947–)

Lentsoane was born in Ga-Marishane, Limpopo, in 1947. Lentsoane took part in many essay-writing competitions in school; his best work from these was published. His talent for poetry developed further in high school, and he was offered a bursary to study at the University of the North (now the University of Limpopo). It was at the university that Lentsoane completed his first collection of poetry in Sepedi. *Direto tša Mang le Mang*, in 1971, the first of a number of literary works. In 2016, Lentsoane was awarded an honorary doctorate for his academic contribution.

Princess Constance Magogo (1900–1984)

Magogo was born into the Zulu royal family, a daughter of King Dinuzulu kaCetshwayo. She was a talented musician, particularly skilled in the traditional instruments isigubhu and isithontolo, and blessed with a beautiful singing voice. Magogo defied discrimination against women by becoming an imbongi, a traditional praise poet, a role usually designated for men. She also performed her music for an audience, unusual for a Zulu woman at the time. She was posthumously awarded the South African National Order of Ikhamanga in Gold for her music compositions in 2003. She was the mother of Mangosuthu Buthelezi, a South African politician and founder of the Inkatha Freedom Party.

BD Magoleng (1935–)

Magoleng is one of the most well-known Setswana authors. Most of his work was published in the 1960s and describes the traditions and culture of the Batswana. Social work and development have a strong influence on his writing. He is the author of *Boka, Ke Boke* (You Recite, and I Recite) and *Losalaba lwa Bomme*, which he wrote with SF Motlhake.

Phorohlo Matheass Mamogobo (1926–2008)

Not much is known about Mamogobo's early years. He matriculated from Botšhabelo Missionary Station, Middelburg and went on to study at Fort Hare University where he received a BA degree. He then obtained a master's degree in Theology from the University of Hamburg in Germany. On his return to South Africa, he taught at a number of schools and colleges. Mamogobo was introduced to English poetry at a young age and quickly developed an interest in it. His writing was influenced by traditional storytelling, while including some Christian themes. Mamogobo is known as one of the first to write modern poetry in Sepedi.

Nontsizi Mgqwetho

Mgqwetho was a South African poet, thought to be the first woman to have written poetry exclusively in isiXhosa. Her work became known through *Umteteli wa Bantu*, a Johannesburg newspaper in which her poems were published between 1920 and 1929. Her poetry is the only isiXhosa poetry to illustrate the life and struggles of an urban Christian black woman, solidifying her place as one of the greatest isiXhosa poets of her time. She was an advocate for women's rights, opposing in many of her works the dominant position men held in the writing of poetry. Her last poem was published in 1929 after which she disappeared from public view. Dr Jeff Opland collected her poetry in a book entitled *The Nation's Bounty: The Xhosa Poetry of Nontsizi Mgqwetho*, published in 2007.

Atwell Sidwell Mopeli-Paulus (1913–1994)

Mopeli-Paulus was born in Lesotho, the son of Sidwel and Manthota Mopeli-Paulus, and a member of the royal family. He studied at Edendale Teachers' College and the University of Witwatersrand where he received a diploma in Bantu Comparative Studies. He joined the Cape Corps at the beginning of the Second World War and served for more than three years as a soldier. He was awarded four medals for bravery during his time in the service. He worked in a lawyer's office and as a teacher after the war. He then became chair of the legislative assembly in Qwaqwa, a separate homeland under the apartheid system, where he eventually became Speaker of the Assembly. He is the author of three collections of Sesotho poetry, but is most known for his novel *Ho Tsamaea Ke Ho Bona* (To Travel is to Learn) and two novels that became classics in English – *Blanket Boy's Moon* (1953) and its equally prestigious follow-up, *Turn to the Dark* (1956).

Samuel Edward Krune Mqhayi (1875–1945)

Mqhayi is often referred to as imbongi yesizwe jikelele (the poet of the nation); he was called "a poet laureate of the African people" by the young Nelson Mandela. He was born in 1875 in Gqumashe, a village in the Eastern Cape. In his youth, he spent six years living in Centane; the knowledge of the Xhosa language and customs that he gained while living there had a great impact on his life and his future writing. In 1897, he launched a newspaper, *Izwi Labantu*, with friends, but his later writings made him a towering figure in isiXhosa literature. His first novel was written in 1907; it was an adaptation of a biblical story and has been lost. This was followed by *Ityala Lamawele* (The Lawsuit of the Twins) and *UDon Jadu* (Don Jadu), translations of both of which are also published in the Africa Pulse series. Mqhayi also published *Imihobe Nemibongo* (1927; Songs of Joy and Lullabies), his first published collection of isiXhosa poems; an autobiography, *UMqhayi wase Ntab'ozuko* (1939; Mqhayi of the Mount of Glory); and another volume of poetry, *Inzuzo* (1942; Reward). He won the 1935 May Ester Bedford Prize. To Enoch Sontonga's hymn "Nkosi Sikelel' iAfrika", now South Africa's national anthem, he added several stanzas. He was the first imbongi to write his poetry down, and it is said that the new words he coined fill many pages of isiXhosa dictionaries.

Christian Themba Msimang (1944–)

Msimang was born in 1944 at the Ethalaneni Mission in Nkandla, KwaZulu–Natal. His aunt was an avid storyteller and told Msimang many stories of his grandfather who fought alongside King Dinuzulu kaCetshwayo in the Anglo-Zulu War (1879). These stories became the basis for his historical novel *Ixili Eladuma eSandlwana* (1979; Stormy Weather Over Isandlwana) years later. He has published novels, poetry collections and plays, among them: *Akuyiwe Emhlahlweni* (1976), *Iziziba zoThukela* (1981), *Folktale Influence on the Zulu Novel* (1986), *Izimbongi Izolo Nanamuhla (Umqulu 1)* (1988), *Izimbongi Izolo Nanamuhla (Umqulu 2)* (1990), *UNodumehlezi kaMenzi* (1990). He won the following awards: BW Vilakazi prize (three times), the De Jager-Raum over-all literary prize, the Shuter & Shooter literary prize for studies in African literature, the De Jager-Raum (Kagiso) Literary Prize for isiZulu in 1995, and the South African Literary Award Chairperson's Award in 2017.

LMS Ngcwabe

Ngcwabe published a slim volume of poetry titled *Khala Zome* (1950) at the Morija printing works in Lesotho and privately distributed it from his home in Roodepoort. It created excitement among readers of isiXhosa and Ngcwabe was described as having unusual talent for his mastery of the technique of writing narrative poems. The book was republished and was quickly reprinted.

Gili kaNobantu

Unfortunately, almost no biographical information for this poet of the isiZulu language could be found. Nobantu seems to be the author of a work entitled *Ekuhambeni*, published by Shuter & Shooter in 1947.

Kemuel Edward Ntsane (1920–1983)

Ntsane was born in Kolojane, Lesotho in 1920. In 1946, he published his first novel, *Masoabi*, and accepted a scholarship to study in the United Kingdom. On his return to Lesotho, Ntsane worked in a number of fields, including as a government archivist and the prime minister's press secretary, while producing a steady stream of literary works in Sesotho: *Mosotho Kajeno* (1946) '*Musa-pelo* (1946), *Bana ba Rona* (1954), *Mmusa-pelo II* (1954), *Josefa le Maria* (1955), *Makumane* (1961), *Nna Sajene Kokobela CID* (1963), *Bao Batho* (1967).

Otty Ezrom Howard Mandlakayise Nxumalo (1938–)

Nxumalo was born in Ngoje, KwaZulu–Natal in 1938. He received a BA (Hons) degree from the University of South Africa, and doctorates from the University of Zululand and Harvard University. He worked for some time as a professor of education at universities in both South Africa and the United States before becoming Director General in the KwaZulu–Natal government. He was also for a time the official speech-writer for King Goodwill Zwelithini, the King of the Zulu nation. Nxumalo is highly regarded and has made great contributions to isiZulu through his many essays, books and poetry. Amongst these are two novellas (*Ikusasa Alaziwa* and *Ngisinga eMpumalanga*) and two volumes of poetry (*Ikhwezi* and *Umzwangedwa*).

Teboho Raboko (1939–)

Very little is known about Teboho Raboko. He was a farmer who spent much of his life working in the mines. Like many miners, he developed a sefela, a self-praising poem in which he introduced himself and his circumstances, adventures, and successes to other miners. The Sesotho sefela included in this anthology was recorded while being performed and later published. The term "sefela" was appropriated by the missionaries to mean a hymn, but has since been broadened and used by contemporary migrants to mean a kind of hymn to the self.

Leetile Disang Raditladi (1910–1971)

Raditladi was born in 1910 in Serowe, Botswana. His talent for writing was recognised early on and his first book was accepted for publication while he was still at school; however the then-Bechuanaland Protectorate (now Botswana) would not allow it to be published. In 1937, Raditladi was banished from his tribe by the regent-king, Kgosi Tshekedi Khama, who accused him of having an affair with Khama's own wife. Thereafter he wrote *Motswasele II* (King Motswasele II), a historical drama that became his most famous work. Its theme is royal despotism and the perverted results of such tyranny. Widely recognised as the pioneering giant of Setswana literature, he published *Sefalana sa Menate* (a collection of poetry that became widely known), another historical drama (*Sekgoma*), and a novel (*Dintshontsho tsa Lorato*). Following Seretse Khama's return to Botswana, Leetile was finally allowed to move back to Serowe in 1957.

Mmapule Emma Ramaila

Ramaila published a short volume of poetry in Sepedi entitled *Dirêtô* in 1956.

Stephen Ratlabala

Ratlabala is the author of *Ditsinkelo tsa Sereti*, as well as *Ithute Direto* with Moses Bopape, both in Sepedi.

Michael Ontefetse Martinus Seboni (1910–1972)

For many years, Seboni was the principal of a school in Nigel, a small mining town in Gauteng. He received a PhD in Education before becoming a Professor of Empirical Education at the University of Fort Hare. He published many literary works in Setswana, and was a playwright and poet. He was also involved in the translation of English literature into Setswana. Seboni is well known for his collection of praise poetry *Maboko*

Maloba le Maabane (Praise Poems Old and New), published in 1949, and *Kgosi Henry wa Bone*, a Setswana translation of Shakespeare's Henry IV.

Bonginkosi Sikhakhane

Sikhakhane was a maskanda singer, a style of music developed in the twentieth century that involves the concertina, guitar, bass, keyboards, vocals and drums. It is a style of Zulu folk music, often containing praise poetry, that was developed by migrant workers in KwaZulu–Natal. Sikhakhane's praise song in isiZulu was recorded by LF Mathenjwa.

Benedict Wallet Vilakazi (1906–1947)

Benedict Vilakazi has been described as the "father of Nguni literature". He was born at the Groutville Mission Station in 1906 and went to school at St Francis College in Mariannhill. He published the first poetry collection in isiZulu, *Inkondlo kaZulu* (Zulu Horizons), regarded as a clear departure from the oral poetic tradition in that language; the volume became world famous through its 1973 English translation by Malcolm and Friedman. While working as a teacher, he obtained a BA degree, and later became the first black South African to lecture white South African students at university level at the University of the Witwatersrand. The isiZulu dictionary he worked on with his colleague CM Doke at the university is still used today. His publications include *Amal'eZulu* (1945), later recognised as one of the 100 best African books of the twentieth century, *Noma Nini* (1935), *Udingiswayo kaJobe* (1939) and *Nje Nempela* (1944). His academic work on the oral tradition earned him a doctorate in 1946, the first to be awarded to a black South African. Only a year later, he died of meningitis at the age of forty-one.

After his death, Vilakazi was awarded the Order of Ikhamanga in Gold for his exceptional contribution to literature in indigenous languages and the preservation of Zulu culture.

St John Page Mbalana Yako (1901–1977)

Yako was born in December 1901, the first of eight children. He earned a Diploma in Agriculture at the Theko School of Agriculture, where he lectured for some time. Yako was known for his love of agriculture and his understanding of its value, especially to a rural community. His works include *Umtha weLanga* (Ray of the Sun) and *Ikhwezi* (Morning Star), both volumes of poetry in isiXhosa.

David Livingstone Phakamile Yali-Manisi (1926–1999)

Yali-Manisi was born in Thembuland, in the Eastern Cape in 1926. He belonged to the amaNcotsho clan, one of the oldest Thembu clans. After matriculating, he worked as a clerk in various government offices until 1982. During this time, his reputation grew as a talented praise singer, and he was chosen to perform at many celebrations. His first publication, a praise poem about Chief Kaiser Mathanzima (leader of the Transkei "homeland"), gained attention after it appeared in the isiXhosa newspaper *Umthunywa* (Messenger). This was followed by the publication of two other works, *Izibongo zeeNkosi zamaXhosa* (Praise Poems on Xhosa Chiefs) and *Inguqu* (Change). Yali-Manisi's poem anthologised here was the first praise poem ever to be written for Nelson Mandela. The imbongi travelled to Johannesburg in 1954 to see this young man of his clan who was creating such a stir in the country. In the light of what happened to Mandela later, Yali-Manisi's poem is shockingly prophetic.

About the translators

Gabeba Baderoon

Gabeba Baderoon was born in Port Elizabeth in 1969 and has a PhD in literature and Women's Studies from the University of Cape Town. She now works as a Women's Studies and African Studies lecturer at Pennsylvania State University in the United States, where she has been for the past ten years. Baderoon has been involved with the translation of poetry from Portuguese to Afrikaans, and from Afrikaans to English. Her volumes of poetry include *The Dream in the Next Body* (2005), *A Hundred Silences* (2006), and *Cinnamon* (2009). She won the Daimler Chrysler Award for South African Poetry (2005), and has had the following fellowships: a Guest Writer Fellowship at the Nordic Africa Institute, a Civitella Ranieri Fellowship (2008), and a Writer's Residency at the University of the Witwatersrand (2008).

Rita Barnard

Born in Pretoria, Rita Barnard is Professor of English and Comparative Literature at the University of Pennsylvania, where she directs the undergraduate program in Comparative Literature. She holds a secondary position as Professor Extraordinaire at the University of the Western Cape. Her books include *The Great Depression and the Culture of Abundance, Apartheid and Beyond: South African Writers and the Politics of Place*, and the edited collection, *The Cambridge Companion to Nelson Mandela*. She was for many years co-editor of *Safundi: The Journal of South African and American Studies*. She has translated poetry and prose to and from English and Afrikaans, and has authored many scholarly articles on questions of translation, language choice, and world literature.

Zukile Jama

Zukile Jama was born in New Brighton, Port Elizabeth in 1962. He is currently an isiXhosa lecturer at the University of the Western Cape, previously holding positions at Vista University (now Nelson Mandela

University), University of Fort Hare, and the University of Cape Town. He has been a member of the isiXhosa National Language Board and the Pan South African Language Board, and is now chair of the Swahili language board of southern Africa.

Fred Khumalo

Fred Khumalo was born in Chesterville outside Durban in 1966, and raised in Mpumalanga township in the KwaZulu–Natal midlands. He obtained a National Diploma in Journalism from the Durban University of Technology before working as a reporter, editor, and columnist for a variety of newspapers. He later obtained a master's in Creative Writing from the University of the Witwatersrand. He has published seven books, including his latest novel *Dancing the Death Drill* (shortlisted for the University of Johannesburg Prize for South African Writing in 2018), and *Bitches' Brew* (joint winner of the European Union Literary Award in 2005). A Nieman Fellow at Harvard University, Khumalo currently lives in Johannesburg where he works as a communications consultant and freelance columnist.

Antjie Krog

Antjie Krog is an Afrikaans poet, writer, journalist and professor at the University of the Western Cape. She was asked to translate the autobiography of Nelson Mandela, *Long Walk to Freedom,* into Afrikaans and in 2002 won the South African Translators' Institute Award for non-fiction. In the same year, she was also awarded the South African Translators' Institute Award for overall outstanding translation for the volume *Met Woorde Soos met Kerse* in which poems of indigenous languages were translated into Afrikaans.

Johannes Malefetsane Lenake

Johan Lenake was born in January 1929 in Frankfort, Orange Free State. After attaining a Primary Teacher's Certificate from Stofberg College in 1949, he started his teaching career at a farm school in Theunissen. Shortly thereafter, he matriculated through private study and in 1952 became an assistant teacher at a community school in Frankfort, rising to the position of principal of the Fouriesburg Bantu community school in 1958. He completed his bachelor's degree through the University of South Africa (UNISA) in 1962 and took up a language assistant post in UNISA's (then) Department of Bantu Languages. In 1979 he was promoted to Senior Lecturer, in 1985 to Associate Professor and in 1987 to full Professor. His doctoral thesis was on the poetry of KE Ntsane. He has written, translated and edited books and manuscripts in Sesotho, English, Afrikaans and isiZulu. He has also won awards for his work from several institutions, such as the African Language Association of South Africa, South African Association of Language Teaching, South African Literary Awards, and Macufe Wordfest in the Free State.

Biki Lepota

Biki Lepota was born in Mpheleng, in the Dennilton area of Limpopo. He started out as a lecturer at the University of Pretoria and worked as a publisher at NB Publishers, before taking a managerial position at the Council on Higher Education. In 2009, Lepota joined Umalusi, Council for Quality Assurance in General and Further Education and Training, as a researcher. He has a wide range of translation experience, working between English and Sepedi. He has participated in various dictionary-making projects, including translating science dictionaries.

David wa Maahlamela

David wa Maahlamela was born in 1984 in Mankweng in Polokwane, Limpopo and is well known as a poet and author. He writes in both Sepedi and English, and has published a novel, *Sejamoledi*, a play, *O Jelwe ke Aretse*, six children's stories, a short story, "The Bus From Cape Town", as well as poetry in a number of anthologies and journals. Maahlamela won the Herifest Prize for Poetry, the Musina Mayoral Excellence Award for Arts development, and the PanSALB Multilingualism Award 2010/2011. Other than his literary works, he has appeared in *Muvhango*, a popular soap opera on SABC2, *Voice of Africa*, a series about South African poets, and SABC News International's *Youth Expression and Africa in Literature*.

Thokozile Mabeqa

Thokozile Mabeqa was born in Alice, Eastern Cape, in 1952. She is now retired but is still involved with academic work at the University of the Western Cape (UWC), where she has lectured on literature, cultural studies, translation, and editing, both in English and isiXhosa. She has a master's degree in translation studies from Stellenbosch University, and another in oral literature from the University of the Western Cape. She began her teaching career in the Eastern Cape, and later moved to a college of education in Cape Town, where she lectured in school management and methods of teaching isiXhosa. She has also taught first-time learners of isiXhosa herself. She was involved in developing an isiXhosa communication curriculum at the Peninsula Technikon (now the Cape Peninsula University of Technology) before moving to UWC. Mabeqa has a wide range of translation experience, from academic texts to national government documents, and has also assisted the Stellenbosch University Language Centre.

Stephen Masote

Stephen Esrom Mosole Masote was born in Meadowlands, Gauteng in 1958. He began his career teaching at high schools in the North West and Gauteng Provinces, later earning his BA (Hons) and master's degrees at the University of Pretoria. In 2009, he moved to the Central University of Technology, Free State, lecturing in Education and Setswana, but in 2014 he joined the University of South Africa (UNISA) where he focused on teaching and assessment. It was at UNISA that he began, and gained a wide experience in, translating. In 2017, he was awarded his PhD from the University of Pretoria. He is currently a senior lecturer for Setswana in the Department of African Languages, UNISA.

Loyiso Mletshe

Loyiso Mletshe was born in Port Elizabeth in 1959. He is currently the head of the isiXhosa Department at the University of the Western Cape, where he has been both a senior lecturer and a student. He has been involved with translating documents for the Western Cape government, and has undertaken a number of projects translating school textbooks and academic material into isiXhosa.

Tšepiso Samuel Mothibi

Tšepiso Samuel Mothibi was born in Alberton, south of Johannesburg in 1981, but grew up in Lesotho. When Mothibi was a child, his interest in translation and language, specifically etymology, was sparked by an Afrikaans cartoon in a South African newspaper. He enjoyed the cartoon, although he could not understand it. He has been writing poetry from the age of 13 and hopes to publish some of his work in the future. He currently works as a copy editor and columnist for *The Post* newspaper in Lesotho, having previously worked as a general handyman and construction site manager.

JC (Koos) Oosthuysen

Koos Oosthuysen was born in Port St Johns, Pondoland in 1933 where he grew up speaking both isiXhosa and Afrikaans. His family moved to Mthatha where he attended an Afrikaans-medium primary school, but his high school education was in English as there were no Afrikaans high schools nearby. This made him fluent in isiXhosa, Afrikaans, and English. Oosthuysen has an honours degree in Philosophy from the University of Stellenbosch and a master's in Theology from Yale University. On his return to South Africa from the United States, he became a minister for isiXhosa-speaking congregations around Stellenbosch, where he was also involved in teaching the language, translating the Bible into isiXhosa, and creating a more functional isiXhosa orthography. In 2013, Oosthuysen was awarded a PhD in African Languages by Rhodes University. Sun Media have since published his work *The Grammar of isiXhosa* in both English and isiXhosa; its innovation is to describe isiXhosa in its own right, freeing it from preconceptions derived from European languages. He is now involved with the Hope Prison Ministry, as well as translation and editing work.

Ncedile Saule

Ncedile Saule was born in Fort Beaufort (eXokoxa) in 1952. Studying first at the University of Fort Hare and then at the University of South Africa (UNISA), he obtained a doctorate. After lecturing isiXhosa at UNISA from 1982 to 2013, he moved to Nelson Mandela University. As a scholar and as a lecturer, he has focused on the work of SEK Mqhayi. He is well-known as an isiXhosa scholar, poet, and historian, but is also the author of six isiXhosa novels, including *Ukhozi Olumphiko* and *Inkululeko Isentabeni*, which won the M-Net Literary Award in 1997 and 2011 respectively. Saule's novel *Unyana Womntu* was adapted for television in 1998 and he has written a number of radio plays.

Nkosinathi Sithole

Nkosinathi Sithole was born in 1975 and grew up in Hlathikhulu near Estcourt, KwaZulu–Natal. He studied at the Universities of the Witwatersrand and KwaZulu–Natal, and has a PhD in English Studies. He has taught at universities in KwaZulu–Natal, and is currently an associate professor of Literature Studies and Creative Writing at the University of the Western Cape. Translation formed an important part of Sithole's postgraduate studies, which included the translation of hymns and stories from isiZulu. His debut novel, *Hunger Eats a Man*, won the Barry Ronge Fiction Award in 2016.

To view the translators speaking about the Africa Pulse series, visit
www.youtube.com/oxfordsouthernafrica

Acknowledgements

Bereng, DCT: **"Lithothokiso tsa Moshoeshoe le tse ling"** from *Lithothokiso tsa Moshoeshoe le tse Ling*, Morija Sesotho Book Depot, 1931. Reprinted by permission of N Sekhonyana Bereng (son of the author).

Bopape, M and Ratlabala, S: **"Polokong"** from *Ithute Direto*, Van Schaik, 1967. Use of "Polokong" by permission of Via Afrika Publishers.

Jolobe, JJR: **"Ukwenziwa komkhonzi"** from *Umyezo*, Wits University Press, Johannesburg, 1951.

Khaketla, BM: **"Ntoa ea Jeremane (1914)"** from *Lipshamathe*, Afrikaanse Pers Boekhandel, Johannesburg, 1950. Reprinted by permission of Dr Mamphono Khaketla (daughter of the author).

Kitchin, MS: **"Go nwela ga Mendi"** from *Boswa jwa Puo* by JM Lekgetho, Pula Press, Gaborone, 1971.

Kitchin, NH: **"Morena Maledu (Cecil Rhodes)"** from *Boswa jwa Puo* by JM Lekgetho, Pula Press, Gaborone, 1971.

Kunene, MR: **"Igama lephoyisa uSwanepuli"** from *Umzwilili wama-Afrika*, Kagiso, Pretoria, 1996; and **"Incwadi kaMandela kuNomzamo, esejele iminyaka engamashumi amabili nane"** from *Indida Yamancasakazi*, Reach Out, Pietermaritzburg, 1995. Reprinted by permission of Mrs Mathabo Kunene, Executive Managing Trustee, Mazisi Kunene Foundation Trust.

Lekhela, EP and Seboni, MOM: **"Sempe a Lešoboro"** from *iBoka Sentle*, Via Afrika, 1970. Use of "Sempe a Lešoboro" by permission of Via Afrika Publishers.

Lentsoane, HML: **"Laboraro le lesoleso"** from *Ihlo la Moreti*, Van Schaik, 1981. Use of "Laboraro le lesoleso" by permission of Via Afrika Publishers.

Magogo, C: **"Ngibambeni, ngibambeni"** and **"Umqhubansuku"** from *The Zulu songs of Princess Constance Magogo KaDinuzulu*. Reprinted by permission of Mangosuthu Buthelezi (son of the author).

Magoleng, BD: **"Mogokgo yo sa rateng tiro"** from *Losalaba lwa Bomme*, Shuter & Shooter, Pietermaritzburg, 1983. Reprinted by permission of Shuter & Shooter.

Mamogobo, P: **"Pheladi"** from *Leduleputswa*, Afrikaanse Pers Boekhandel, 1953.

Mgqwetho, N: **"Imbongikazi NoAbantu Batho"**, **"Ingxoxo yomginwa kumagqoboka!"**, and **"Umbhinqo weAfrika!"**. Copies of the three poems by Nontsizi Mgqwetho are housed in *The Opland Collection of Xhosa Literature* and are used by kind permission of Jeff Opland.

Mopeli-Paulus, AS: **"Moafrika"** from *Ho Tsamaea Ke Ho Bona*, Lesotho, Morija Sesotho Book Depot, 1945.

Mqhayi, SEK: **"A! Silimela!"** appeared on a 78rpm recording released in 1934; a copy of the recording is housed in *The Opland Collection of Xhosa Literature*.

The text was published in "Two Unpublished Poems by SEK Mqhayi" by Jeff Opland, published in *Research in African Literatures*, vol. 8, no. 1, 1977, pp. 27–53, reprinted as "Two Recorded Poems by SEK Mqhayi" in *Xhosa Literature: Spoken and Printed Words* by Jeff Opland, University of KwaZulu–Natal Press, Pietermaritzburg, 2018, pp. 48–72. The text is reprinted here by kind permission of Jeff Opland; **"Aa! Zweliyazuza, itshawe laseBhilitani!"** from *Inzuzo* by SEK Mqhayi, Wits University Press, 1957; and **"Ukutshona kukaMendi"**, and **"Umkhosi wemiDaka"** from *Ityala Lamawele: Namanye Amabali AkwaXhosa* by SEK Mqhayi, Lovedale Press, 1931.

Msimang, CT: **"Uthando"** and **"Uze ungiphuzise amanzi"** from *Iziziba zoThukela*, Via Afrika, Pretoria, 1980. Reprinted by permission of the author.

Ngcwabe, LMS: **"Ukufa"** from *Khala Zome*, Bona Press, Johannesburg, 1950.

kaNobantu, G: **"Ingodusi"** from *Ekuhambeni*, Shuter & Shooter, Pietermaritzburg, 1947.

Ntsane, KE: **"Mohokare (Caledon River)"** and **"Moratuwa"** from *'Musa-pelo*, Morija Sesotho Book Depot, 1978. Reprinted by permission of Chaka Ntsane (son of the author).

Nxumalo, OEHM: **"Lisholani?"**. Reprinted by permission of the author.

Raboko, T: **"Sefela"** from *Lifela tsa Litsamaea-naha poetry: A literary analysis* by Makali IP Mokitimi. Van Schaik, Pretoria, 1998. Reprinted by permission of Van Schaik Publishers.

Raditladi, LD: **"Aferika"**, **"Dingana le Maburu"**, **"Kgosi Tshaka"**, **"Ntwa ya 1939–45"** and **"Pula"** from *Sefalana sa Menate*, Van Schaik, Pretoria, 2000.

Ramaila, ME: **"Modjadji"** from *Direto*, Van Schaik, 1956. Use of "Modjadji" by permission of Via Afrika Publishers.

Ratlabala, S: see above at Bopape, M.

Seboni, MOM and Lekhela, EP: see above at Lekhela, EP.

Sikhakhane, B: **"Izibongo zikamaskandi"** from "An analysis of Maskandi poetry as a genre of South African Poetry", by Mathenjwa, LF, MA thesis, University of Zululand, 1997.

Vilakazi, BW: **"Impophoma yeVictoria"** from *Inkondlo kaZulu*, Wits University Press, 1965; and **"Nomkhosi kababa"** from *Noma Nini*, Wits University Press, 1962.

Yako, St J PM: **"Ukufinyezwa nokubiywa komhlaba"** from *Umtha weLanga*, Lovedale Press, Alice, 1958.

Yali-Manisi, DLP: **"UNkosi Rholihlahla Nelson Mandela (Aa! Zweliyashukuma!)"** from *Xhosa literature: spoken and printed words*, by Jeff Opland, University of KwaZulu–Natal Press, Pietermaritzburg, 2018. Reprinted by permission of Jeff Opland and Busisiwe Yali-Manisi (daughter of the author) on behalf of the literary estate of the author.